The Making of a Civilian Soldier in the Civil War

The Making of a Civilian Soldier in the Civil War

The First Diary of Private William J. McLean Along the Chesapeake & Ohio Canal and the Affair at Edwards Ferry

Written and Edited by
Dennis D. Urban

Washington DC

Copyright © 2019 by Dennis D. Urban
New Academia Publishing, 2019

All rights reserved. No part of this book may be reproduced or transmitted in any form or by any means, electronic or mechanical, including photocopying, recording, or by any information storage and retrieval system.

Printed in the United States of America

Library of Congress Control Number: 2019908166
ISBN 978-1-7326988-6-4 paperback (alk. paper)

 An imprint of New Academia Publishing

 4401-A Connecticut Ave., NW #236 - Washington DC 20008
info@newacademia.com - www.newacademia.com

To my father, Leonard L. Urban Sr. (1905 - 1991),
who first ignited my interest in the Civil War
with a trip to Gettysburg
when I was a young elementary school student.

Contents

Illustrations, Images, and Maps	viii
Preface	ix
Acknowledgements	xii
Introduction: Knowing William J. McLean	1
Chapter I: The Search for the Diarist	7
Chapter II: The Early Life and War Service of William, John, and Simpson McLean	15
Chapter III: Antebellum Herkimer County, Fairfield, and Fairfield Seminary (Academy)	29
Diary	33
Chapter IV: May 1861; Enlistment and Mustering	35
Chapter V: June 1861; Albany Experiences and Orders to Travel	43
Chapter VI: July 1861; Washington City and the Aftermath of Bull Run	49
Chapter VII: August 1861; Camp Jackson, Darnestown, and Preparing for Action	65
Chapter VIII: September and Early October 1861; First Action, Incursion into Virginia	85
Chapter IX: The Affair at Edwards Ferry	111
Chapter X: Correcting the Official Records	121
Chapter XI: The Post-War Years of the McLean Family	133
Epilogue	151
Works Cited and Sources	153
About the Author	155

Illustrations, Images, and Maps

Thirty-Fourth New York Memorial Pin	7
Harewood Hospital, Washington City, circa 1864	23
Fairfield Seminary, Fairfield, New York	32
Map of Fairfield, NY, circa 1865	32
Captain Thomas Corcoran, Company C (post-war image)	36
Tweddle Hall exterior, circa 1876	40
Tweddle Hall Assembly area	40
Washington City map, circa 1860	52
Kalorama Mansion, burned, circa 1865	54
White House, south view, from CDV	55
Diary pages for July 17 – July 20	56
Albert Easterbrook image in newly issued uniform	60
Map showing location of Tennallytown	61
Water Works at Great Falls, MD, circa 1861-1865	64
Typical Countersign picket note	66
Seneca Mills camp location, Montgomery County, MD	67
Envelope addressed by Solomon Clark	71
Ezra Fenton image and bible verse	74
Map: Darnestown to Camp Jackson, Montgomery County, MD	103
Map: Darnestown, MD	104
Map: Ball's Bluff area showing Edwards Ferry and Conrad's Ferry	112
General Stone's Division at Edwards Ferry, October 20, 1861	114
Goose Creek entering the Potomac River, Virginia shore	115
Edwards Ferry looking across to Goose Creek from the Maryland shore	115
Artillery fire at Edwards Ferry, October 22, 1861	119
Retreat of Union Forces, October 23, 1861	120
William J. McLean and Simpson McLean, circa 1912	145
34th New York Infantry Reunion Ribbon, September 17, 1918	151

Preface

Every Civil War soldier who kept a diary had a story to tell and each felt his story was important enough to record the events for himself, for family members, or for his own future remembrance of his experiences. These young men were not professional writers or even experienced writers, but they had a sense of history. They knew they were involved in something significant in the history of the nation. From family stories and perhaps even directly from family members they were aware that the struggle for independence had taken place a mere 85 years ago. More recently, the war with Mexico had touched the lives of some of their fathers and other relatives.

This was their opportunity to record firsthand the next chapter in the history of the nation. Tens of thousands seized this opportunity and recorded their observations and adventures in diaries, through correspondence with newspapers back home, and by letters to family and friends. Many of these writings have been lost to history. Thankfully, many have also survived. They survived in family archives and were cherished by family members. Perhaps they were periodically taken out by the veterans themselves and re-read for their own memory refreshment. On other occasions, these texts were probably read to children or grandchildren, and given to relatives who kept the family history. Other veterans turned their multiple diaries and letters into manuscripts to be kept for future generations. As veterans began to die off later in the 19th century, their writings became the basis of regimental histories and books. This was also the period in which monuments began to be erected on battlefields as another way to remember their experiences, their struggles, and their long-departed comrades.

This is one such unique story which also deserves to be told and remembered.

This book is so much more than a mere transcription of a Civil War diary. In fact, the diary transcription only encompasses Chapters IV through VIII. The balance of the book before and after tells the story of an American family with two sons and a father who served the Union in the American Civil War. Such extensive service within one family is somewhat unusual. The fact that they all survived the conflict and lived long and fruitful lives is also unusual and speaks to the success of the American dream; a dream for which the father, John C. McLean, first emigrated to America.

Much can be gleaned about the diary writer by leaving the transcription in the manner in which it was originally written. I have endeavored to do that throughout the transcription. While William McLean was reasonably well-educated, his use of proper sentence structure, punctuation, capitalizations or lack thereof, and spelling left much to be desired by modern standards. Nonetheless, he is easily understood. He uses his own abbreviations for days of the week and for an unexplained two letter code which may have designated the weather conditions of the day. In a few places, he used a small drawing or symbol at the end of a sentence to perhaps signify his thought at the time he wrote. All of this has been left as written. Undecipherable words are indicated by a blank underline.

I also added annotated information in between some of the diary entries to provide historic information to explain what the diarist wrote. In some locations, I quote from other works or add previously published or unpublished letters to further interpret an incident or event. When quoting unpublished letters, I maintained the original spacing, spelling, and punctuation for context. In most instances, these letters are taken from my personal collection and they disclose previously unknown facts about an incident. I made liberal use of maps, prints and period images to add context to the story. Several of the images are published here for the first time. Taken together, these additions complete the story and add to our history and understanding of the events of war as experienced by the common soldier.

Footnotes are at the bottom of each page, many of which relate to a soldier, friend, or relative mentioned by name in the diary. The use of ( ) next to a name throughout the text and primarily in the footnotes indicates the age of the individual. In such cases, I use a note to explain who this person was and how they may have known William. One such mention of a young lady to whom William wrote became his wife after his service concluded. Indeed it was not unusual for love to blossom between a soldier and a girl back home.

Finally, any errors of omission or commission are totally mine and for which I accept complete responsibility. I believe they are few. I hope the reader gets to know and appreciate the life of William John McLean and his family as I did.

Acknowledgements

No book is written in a vacuum. While a single individual is usually responsible for the writing and editing, significant help along this path is given by many individuals. It takes many years of painstaking diligence and research to make a work such as this possible. I have many people to thank and acknowledge.

First and foremost is Brian Green, Kernersville, NC, who told me of the existence of the diary more than 20 years ago in February, 1998. His relating of the soldier's description of the Washington City area and his travels along the Chesapeake and Ohio Canal caught my attention and I purchased the diary from him sight unseen. Thus began a research and writing odyssey which culminated with the publication of this work.

Shortly after I transcribed the diary into handwritten pages, David P. Krutz of Little Falls, NY, very kindly spent several days with me touring the Herkimer County and Little Falls area as I examined the places that were important in the life of William J. McLean. Through the immense courtesy of David I saw and photographed the site of Fairfield Academy. Unfortunately, all the buildings were long gone and only a historic marker remained. Just seeing the then empty ground where McLean trod made his life real for me. David kindly drove me to several areas important in the history of the 34th New York. We finished our tour in Little Falls where I saw the still extant park at which the 34th had their welcoming ceremony. A highlight for me was viewing and examining artifacts of the 34th at the 1833 bank building which serves as the Little Falls Historical Society Museum. David is the treasurer of the Little Falls Historical Society. Holding an Enfield musket carried by a member of the 34th was an experience I never forgot. A few years later, in October, 2002, I met David and members of the Captain Henry Galpin Civil

War Roundtable in Sharpsburg, MD, where I was able to return his favor by providing the group, which contained at least one descendent of the 34th, a tour of the Antietam battlefield. Our tour that day began at the memorial to the 34th on a hill just a few yards north of the Dunker Church. This memorial marks the furthest advance of the 34th into the West Woods area. I am forever grateful for the courtesies David extended to me.

The Herkimer County Historical Society provided me with background information on the history of the county and the region.

James A. Morgan III, a wonderful author, historian, researcher, and friend, whose book about the battle of Ball's Bluff and Edwards Ferry, I quote in a later chapter of this book, spent a day with me on those fields which he knows so intimately. Walking the area where the 34th landed at Goose Creek and spent many wondering and perhaps terrifying hours anticipating an attack made their experiences real for me. I truly felt their presence here. I remain indebted to Jim.

I was helped along the way by several unnamed staff at the National Archives who helped a neophyte researcher navigate the mysteries of microfilm as I narrowed my search to identify the diarist. Their help and suggestions greatly aided my research which ended in success.

This book would not have been possible without the most capable and continuing assistance of Courtney Davis. As I was seeking assistance to turn my handwritten transcribed pages into a word document of the diary, I asked Dr. Aaron Astor, author and history professor at Maryville College, Maryville, TN, if he could ask in his classes if someone might be interested in assisting me in this project. Graduating senior, Courtney Davis, volunteered without knowing what was in the offing. I am indebted to Aaron for his willingness to help my project along. Over many meetings, I entrusted Courtney with my handwritten pages and she ably turned them into the document I desired, while she adhered to the integrity of the diary as written by William McLean. It was vitally important to maintain his imperfect spelling, punctuation, capitalization, and abbreviations. Courtney did this with immense accuracy. Recently, Courtney assisted with the final editing and manual of style issues which required more than my eyes and abilities could provide. Through this journey together, Courtney became and remains a trusted friend. I am forever in her debt and I hope this experience inspires her in a positive way in her future endeavors.

Finally, my utmost appreciation to Private William J. McLean for his diligence in writing the diary which inspired my curiosity and drove me to know more about this young patriot.

Dennis D. Urban
Oak Ridge, TN
March, 2019

Introduction
Knowing William J. McLean

William J. McLean was no different than thousands of young men and boys who enlisted at the start of the Civil War in April, 1861. The reasons which enticed these young recruits to join were numerous and not likely limited to a single justification. Perhaps it was dissatisfaction with their current state in life or a sense of adventure that moved them to enlist. Maybe it was the promise of a bounty from the state and/or the Federal government along with a salary for two years which would provide a source of income for their spouses and families. It even could have been the collective enthusiasm and war fever generated by newspapers, orators, and their friends and acquaintances which influenced a "group" enlistment. After all, on April 15, 1861, President Abraham Lincoln called for 75,000 volunteers to put down the rebellion by the South. The coming fury had to be actively discussed within the large student body of Fairfield Academy and Seminary in Fairfield, Herkimer County, NY, where William was a student and teacher. In fact, the principal, Rev. J.B. Van Patten, A.M., who was also a professor at Fairfield Seminary, enlisted with the students and became chaplain of the 34th New York Infantry. For others, it may have been under the influence of "John Barleycorn" that they signed their name to the enrollment form. This was not uncommon. For a few, it may have been a sense of duty, obligation, or even patriotism knowing that older family members had previously served their country in the War of 1812 or the recent Mexican War. For most, it was likely a combination of several of these reasons. We do not know William McLean's reasoning because it is not expressed in extant writings. We can, however, infer from what he wrote that he was patriotic. We can also deduce a reasonable picture of his personality and his traits from what he wrote in his first diary and in his post-war letters.

In one of his post-war letters, William described himself as both a student and a teacher at Fairfield Academy (Seminary and Academy are used interchangeably) when he enrolled in the 34th on April 20, 1861. This was just seven days after the surrender of Ft. Sumter. The academy, which began as strictly a medical college, was turned into a co-educational institute circa 1839. At that time it named itself a Classical Academy and Female Collegiate Institute. The school now incorporated a teacher training program and a college preparation curriculum. The enrollment of the academy was 551 in 1861. Such a high enrollment on a large campus with several buildings and dormitories made the academy quite a prominent institution in Herkimer County. On that same day, several of his friends and contemporaries from Fairfield and throughout the Herkimer County area likewise enlisted. Years later, when William first applied for a pension at the age of 39, he described himself as a farmer and a teacher at the time of his military enrollment. Since he was 21 years old, the farmer/teacher scenario is most plausible. According to the Federal census of 1860 for Herkimer County, William was boarding with the Palmer Root family near Poland, NY. This location is about 12 miles from Fairfield. The Root family consisted of the husband, Palmer (57), his wife, Sally (56), plus four grown children, 16 years and older. The farm was a prosperous one with a real estate value of $7,500 and a personal estate value of $6,000 for Palmer and $2,000 for Sally. One of the children was John B. Root (17), who was four years younger than McLean and possibly a student at Fairfield Academy. This association may have been why William ended up living with the Root family. In his first diary, William mentions writing to John Root. Quite possibly, William attended classes and sometimes taught when Fairfield Academy was in session and worked the farm, assisting the Root family, when class was not in session.

A catalogue published in 1894 of literary exercises connected along with the reunions of the Fairfield Seminary Philorhetorean Society (a literary society), identifies William J. McLean as being a member of the society in 1861 and his residence as Utica, NY. To be correct, William was residing in Utica in 1894 but not in 1861. As noted above, William was residing on a farm in Herkimer County with the Root family after his father and brothers moved to Ohio in the late 1850s. Utica is the town in which William spent his final years and where he is buried. However, a pre-war connection may be present as well. If there is one, it remains undetermined. This writer believes the Utica notation in the 1894 catalogue refers to his residence at that time.

McLean was certainly educated, quite literate, and seemed to enjoy writing since he kept a diary throughout his two years of service. His diligence in keeping these diaries indicated he had a sense of history and realized the importance of recording what he saw and did. Indeed, as you shall read, his attention to detail would serve to clear his record almost 50 years later when he sought an increase in his pension! Like many other writers of his day, his punctuation and capitalization left something to be desired. William's sentences were frequently run-on and without ending periods and beginning capitalizations. This style made some of his diary entries difficult to read. Reading a long entry a second time usually determined where the endpoint of the sentence should be. Nonetheless, he was easily understandable. Further, as was typical of the time, spelling could be a challenge. Fellow soldier's names were commonly misspelled as was often true on official records. In such cases, I have relied on the 1903 regimental history roster as the correct spelling. His ability to write was well known in the regiment since he mentions writing letters for several of his friends in his company. His diary entries became longer, more descriptive, and wordier as events became more interesting and he became more adept at writing.

The diary itself is a 4" x 2 ½" embossed, brown leather bound, blank page booklet with a leather tab that fits through a strap on the front cover to keep the booklet closed. It is well-worn from being carried in his knapsack and handled on many more occasions than the few months in which he actually wrote in it. The back cover is separating from the leather covering. William sewed the back cover to the leather with brown thread to keep the book from coming apart. This truly indicates the importance of the diary to the writer. Inside the front covers William kept two lists. The first list is names and amounts which appear to be in cents. The names are members of his regiment to whom he apparently lent money. There are approximately 18 names on this list. The other list appears to be money he made from selling items like his "wach", performing services such as "examining heads" (combing for lice) and money paid him for "soldiering" (his pay).

McLean kept this diary and all his others among his most prized possessions until his death in February, 1922. This diary has about 90 pages; all but a few contain writing. William took pains to number each page in the upper right corner and note the month on the top of each page as well. He not only noted the number of each day but also used an abbreviation to note the day of the week. He began some day's entries with a two letter code which he did not explain but which may have referred to the weather conditions of that day.

William McLean was an accurate and detailed observer of the people and conditions surrounding him. When the regiment went to Albany, he had time to visit the sights around the city; a city he mentioned in the diary that he had visited once before when he was quite young. After the regiment arrived in the nation's capital, William detailed his sightseeing around Washington City. At times, he related exactly where he was and what he was doing as he wrote in the diary; e.g. "I went to the Capitol of the US and was much interested in viewing its halls ec. the paintings and engravings were splendid. I viewed the place till satisfied then I went into the front yeard (sic) or grove and wrote some in my diary, then I lay down a while." When viewing contemporary images of the exterior of the Capitol, one can imagine just where William was as he wrote those words. At other instances, he noted the exact time of day he was writing in the diary. More often than not he went alone on these excursions. William, along with a few others in his regiment, also became active correspondents to the Herkimer County Journal; recounting everything from camp life to encounters with the enemy. These accounts became valuable sources of information for the families and citizens back home.

William had a lot of friends, both male and female, and had an active social life during his three years in Herkimer County preceding his enlistment. Many friends and fellow students enlisted with him while others remained at home. He wrote to, and received letters from, both men and women he knew before the war. William wrote to some of the fathers of his contemporaries and to older men with whom he was associated. He had a trusting relationship with Leonard A. Brockett to whom he sent money for safekeeping. However, it has not been determined how William knew Leonard Brockett. Brockett was a 33-year-old widowed farmer living near Salisbury, NY, which is just a few miles from Fairfield. His 150 acre farm was valued at $9,000 in 1860, making him a very prosperous farmer in the area. His household consisted of two young sons, two female "servants" and a farm laborer. Additionally, one of the women to whom William wrote was to become his first wife after his period of service was completed. His first diary, however, does not offer any hint of affection. Perhaps such affection was to develop over the time of his letter writing as happened with so many soldiers. Such romantic feelings, developed through letter writing, were quite common with Civil War soldiers.

Within his regiment McLean was both an entrepreneur and a salesman. He was quite industrious during his time of service in the regiment. He bought and sold items including some items that he was given or that he brought with him. He mentions selling a watch and a pistol within the first few months of his service. He made money by "examining heads" which was likely the examining and combing of lice from the heads of his fellows. When on picket duty or otherwise away from camp, he collected fruit or vegetables and brought them back to sell to his camp mates. He recorded the money he gained from his sales and he lent money to his friends in the regiment. His first diary records 18 such loans. He was likeable enough to strike up conversations and make friends with those he met while picketing and exploring along the Chesapeake and Ohio Canal. He was not shy about requesting a meal from those he met; then offering to pay for it. At one point William is admonished by a local white man for socializing with his "negros" as this was against the social mores of the time.

Finally, William McLean was a Christian, attending the religious oriented academy in Fairfield. At various times in his first diary he makes the mark of a Christian cross but does not explain why he has done so. He never divulges his specific faith association. McLean's political leanings seemed to be towards the Republican Party. On one occasion, he mentions having previously attended a "Wide Awake" meeting. The Wide Awakes affiliated with the Republican Party and they were a paramilitary campaign organization. A group called the "Wide Awakes" existed in New York City in the 1850's and was loosely associated with the Know Nothing movement. William does not refer to the Know Nothings so we cannot assume that he agreed with their sentiments.

All in all, William McLean was an educated, literate, and socially active young man who was an interested observer of the events of the period. He went to war with many of his compatriots, all filled with the enthusiasm of youth, not knowing for how long and having no conception of the horrors they would endure. While his experiences were not significantly different from others of his time, he nonetheless recognized the importance of recording his story for himself, for his family, and for future generations. Therefore, it is important that his story be told.

Chapter I

The Search for the Diarist

34th New York Memorial Pin

A diary is a recording of daily life events written by and important primarily to its author. The content is usually very mundane and innocuous. However, in the case of Civil War soldier's diaries, the content can be of historic first hand events experienced by the soldier. With the passage of time, what may have seemed as ordinary events could become important snippets of history.

Many Civil War soldiers on both the Union and Confederate sides kept diaries. They were cherished throughout the lifetime of the soldier and later by his family and future generations. They became a part of the family history. Many identified and unidentified diaries survive today. It is rare that a surviving but unidentified Civil War diary can be identified with ironclad certainty to a specific writer. This is one of those rare stories.

The diary was originally identified to the 62nd New York Infantry regiment and the writer was unknown. I purchased it because of its content about the Washington, DC area; the area in which I was raised and spent the better part of my life. The diary contains detailed descriptions of visits by the writer to the US Capitol and to the White House. The writer talks about his camp (Camp Kalorama) in Washington, DC, and tells of some of his adventures while at that location; including the story of a "zouave shot last n(ight) at a whorehouse...the boys to have revenge burnt it to the ground." During the Civil War years, what is now known in Washington City as the Federal Triangle was an area filled with dilapidated shanties which served as houses of prostitution. Later, the writer described the cavalry charging down the street with their sabers drawn to break up groups of soldiers gathered in the area and his jumping over a fence to avoid them. He also tells of marching from Camp Kalorama up the Potomac River along the Chesapeake and Ohio Canal to Seneca, MD, and of his picket duty, local sightseeing visits, and adventures along the canal. All of these descriptions were of immense interest to me because I knew these areas well and had often walked them.

I was even more intrigued by whom the writer might be. This was the soldier's first diary after enlisting so he was detailed about recording his adventures. But he failed to write his name in the front of the diary or anywhere else in it, as one might expect he would. After reading and manually transcribing almost every word of the diary, I made it my mission to determine, if possible, the identity of the diarist. Little did I know at the time that this would be an eighteen month odyssey with numerous dead ends and non-productive leads.

My search began with confirmation of the identification of the New York unit to which the diarist belonged. However, the 62nd New York just didn't fit the beginning time frame. The writer began this first diary the day he left with other recruits, May 6, 1861, to travel to Albany, NY, for their mustering. According to *Dyer's Compendium* the 62nd was organized at New York City, not Albany. Dates mentioned in the diary did not fit to the 62nd either. The muster in date of June 15, 1861, and the departure date from Albany of July 3 fit only to the 34th New York Infantry, the Herkimer

Regiment. The regiment was named for their county of origin (a common practice for many regiments) in New York. I had easily identified the regiment. Now the real work began.

As I transcribed the diary into over eighty handwritten pages, I reached several conclusions. The diarist was young, possibly a student or a teacher at a school, with the rank of Private during the five plus months this diary covered. Additionally, he never referenced his marital status but he had a circle of acquaintances both male and female with whom he regularly exchanged correspondence. He recorded the names of those to whom he wrote and those from whom he received letters. He wrote to his parents but never mentioned them by name. Several people were mentioned only by their first name. He often mentioned activities with his fellow soldiers, identifying them by name, but never mentioning his or their company letter designation. I realized the search was not to be an easy one and one that may prove impossible.

Since I was certain that the diary belonged to a soldier of the 34th New York Infantry, I obtained a reprinted copy of the regimental history. The history contained an excellent alphabetical general roster of all of the original enlistees and all those who served in the regiment, their complete names (sometimes with middle name or initial), age at enlistment, their date and place of their enlistment, plus the company to which they belonged. I counted 1,008 names in the complete roster. The roster also contained specific information on the location of the formation of the first companies. The town of Fairfield, NY, and Fairfield Academy were mentioned within the first dates entered in the diary. With his first entry on May 6, the diarist mentioned Fairfield ("I got a revolver presented to me at Fairfield") and three other towns in the vicinity of Fairfield through which he passed. Using this information, I established some parameters to begin the identification process.

First, I made a list of all the fellow soldiers he mentioned by full name and recorded the company to which each belonged. The vast majority of these individual belonged to Company C, so I theorized that the diarist was likely a member of this company. Reading through the regimental enlistees, I made a list of all non-officer enlistees under the age of twenty-six (an arbitrarily age I selected) who enlisted May 1, 1861, (the diarist's enlistment date) at Fairfield and several of the nearby towns. The regimental rolls were rapidly filled since no enrollments for these towns were listed between May 2nd and May 6th, the regiment's departure date. This initial list encompassed 38 names. Next, I could eliminate those fellow soldiers he mentioned by name in the diary. I also eliminated the musicians because musicians would not usually have served on picket duty which was described by the diarist. My list was reduced to 22 soldiers. Then, I made another list of all the people he named to whom he wrote including father, mother, relatives, and friends. This list totaled 20 names. I noted how many times he wrote to each individual. Most of the people to whom he wrote were mentioned by first and last name. A few were mentioned by their first initials and included their surname. He mentioned writing to "father" and "brother" as well as to an "Uncle John". Curiously, one person was mentioned only as "Simpson" with no other clue as to the identity of the person. He never mentioned a town or place name for any of those to whom he wrote.

Upon reading my transcription again, I noted that on September 22, 1861, the diarist wrote "a let(ter) to father respecting Simpson's coming to enlist in our Co(mpany)." This notation sent me back to the regimental roster, searching for anyone with the first name, middle name, or surname of Simpson. Unexpectedly, I found none. This was the first dead end of many to follow.

My search began in earnest and with determination by accessing several of the 22 individual soldier's military and pension records (from my list of possibilities) from the National Archives. Fortunately I lived in the Washington area at that time and could easily travel to the Archives. About this time, I realized that I had no idea if the diarist had survived the war. If there was no pension record I may never be able to identify the diarist. I would have to read through the individual records I selected for clues which may link a soldier to information in the diary. While I selected 26 years old as the upper age bracket of my soldier, I felt that he was somewhat younger than that. Using a Herkimer County map, I chose to examine the records of soldiers who enlisted at Fairfield or a nearby town and their age being 26 or less. Over a period of several months, I accessed and copied the records of five arbitrary but potential choices. All of these candidates had survived the war but none of their records contained a clue that could be tied back to the diary. Now I had five more dead ends. I realized that my search may never reach the desired result.

As one of my second round of arbitrary possibilities I selected a 20-year-old soldier named William J. McLean who, according to the regimental roster, enlisted in Company C on May 1, 1861, at Fairfield. As I began to read through his military records at the National Archives in Washington, DC, I noted that these records said he "enrolled May 1 at Albany". The regimental history showed that the 34th went to Albany, but they had not arrived until several days after May 1. The regimental history further showed that several soldiers had enrolled at Fairfield or at other towns close to Fairfield but they were all mustered in at Albany. This notation in the records would prove to be an error. I knew from previous research that such notations in official military records were not always accurate.

As I read further in his records, I noted that McLean was wounded December 13, 1862, at Fredericksburg, VA. Later muster rolls and regimental returns placed him at the Hammond General Hospital at Point Lookout, MD, in November and December, 1862, and at the Turner's Lane General Hospital, Philadelphia, PA, in January and February, 1863. A muster roll for March and April, 1863, listed McLean as "deserted from the US service March 13, 1863." By April 10, 1863, he appeared on the muster roll of Captain Schmitt's 2nd Division, Convalescents, New York Volunteers stationed near Alexandria, VA. It did not make sense to me that if he deserted in March he would be in a convalescent regiment in early April. Yet his company muster out roll on June 30, 1863, reported him as a deserter in March and returned to his regiment June 9, 1863. At least I now knew that McLean had survived the war and later applied for a pension. A further notation in his pension file from 1886 said the charge of desertion of March 13, 1863, is removed and that McLean was absent without proper authority from March 14, 1863, to June 9, 1863. A subsequent notation in February, 1913, stated that the charge of desertion was erroneous. This was an issue for which I hoped to find an explanation.

Reading further through the records I saw a letter from McLean dated October 25, 1912, to the Commissioner of Pensions stating that his pension rate of $21.50 per month was incorrect and that it should be $23.00. The reply to this letter stated that "you were absent without proper authority two months and twenty five days". Next followed a series of letters from William McLean to the pension board detailing how he was transferred from the hospital at Point Lookout, MD, to the Philadelphia hospital based on an error by the Wardmaster at Point Lookout. McLean wrote,

> I can give an account of myself every day from May 6, 1861 when we (our Regt) went to Albany NY to drill until the 30th day of June 1863. I have a written diary of every day.... The Wardmaster got mixed at this & gave in my name as a Penn(sylvania) soldier...I was in no way to blame in having my name mixed in where it dident belong. But I was very anxious for the change. Philadelphia had been my home & I had many friends there...My Wardmaster learned his mistake & came to me & told me I had no right to go & he would have to hold me back. We had some very hot words (I think he feared me). However he dident try to prevent my going he gave me a pass card as he did to the rest of the ward...To cover up his mistake when the boat had gone he reported me missing this was Feb 13th 1863.

"I can give an account of myself every day from May 6, 1861...I have a written diary of every day." I could scarcely believe what I was reading. My diary began on May 6, 1861. However, I quickly realized that other soldier's diaries could have begun on this same date. I had to find additional evidence before I could be certain that William McLean was my diarist. The Commissioner of Pensions, J.L. Davenport, had answered McLean on April 3, 1913, and asked him to supply additional information to substantiate his claim. McLean wrote back on April 12 and related a family history for which he had a remarkable memory. Part of what he wrote on that letter is as follows:

> My Father was a mover (and) he moved eleven times between 1846 and 1858...in Feb(ruary) 1858 he went to the state of Ohio and lived near painsville. I dident go to Ohio

with the family. I stayed in NY so as to attend the schools as I had & I studied & taught till sumpter fell & then I went to the front from Fairfield Academy Herkimer Co NY. My father and brother enlisted in the 29 Ohio Regt in 1861 & my brother was 5 years and 1-1/2 months younger than I.

Reading this while sitting in a National Archives research room made the hair on the back of my neck stand up. A chill swept through my body and I felt like shouting out loud. I hastened to copy the full file so I could hurry back to the microfilm room and access the Ohio regimental files. There I found a 44-year-old John C. McLean and an 18-year-old Simpson McLean who had both enlisted in Company F of the 29th Ohio late in the fall of 1861. Here was the ironclad proof I needed. Because I now found the identity of Simpson to be William's brother, I had identified my diarist beyond a shadow of a doubt!

Further records checks revealed that William's father, John C. McLean, had a short two month term of service before being discharged for disability in November, 1862. No record of him existed beyond that point. He apparently did not apply for a pension. Simpson McLean survived the war after being wounded three times, once severely. He was wounded for the first time at Cedar Mountain (August 9, 1862), seriously wounded at Culp's Hill in Gettysburg (July 3, 1863), and for the third time at Stone Mountain, GA (June 16, 1864). While Simpson's enlistment record showed him as an 18-year-old, William's notation in one of his letters of his brother being 5-1/2 years younger than he revealed that Simpson was actually only 16 years old when he enlisted. He obviously lied with the knowledge and approval of his father and enlisted a month and a half after his father. One can surmise that Simpson had to get the approval of his mother to enlist or that Simpson simply ran away to enlist. His father kept his secret and did not send him back home. After their service, both John and Simpson McLean eventually went back to Herkimer County, NY, where Simpson obtained an invalid pension and lived out his final years close to his brother, William. Simpson died September 5, 1913, at the age of 68.

Once his records were corrected, William J. McLean successfully earned the additional pension he sought. It was through his diaries and because of his wonderful memory that he was able to successfully build his case. The mistake of being recorded as a Pennsylvania soldier and sent to a Philadelphia hospital, and the record of desertion to cover the error, became the key components in solving the mystery. William's very detailed letters describing how these events occurred allowed me to identify the diarist with certainty. After returning from his term of service, William spent the rest of his life in Herkimer and Fulton counties, where he outlived two of his three wives and fathered nine children between 1864 and 1889. At the time of his death on February 22, 1922, at the age of 82, he resided in Utica, NY. He rests there today as an honored veteran whose story of perseverance and fortitude is cherished by this writer.

Chapter II

The Early Life and War Service of William, John, and Simpson McLean

Private William J. McLean, Company C, 34th New York Infantry

William John McLean was born January 15, 1840, at or near Philadelphia, PA. His father, John C. McLean emigrated from Scotland some years before William's birth and was 26 years old when William was born. William was his first born child. His mother, Hannah, died in February, 1852, just after William turned 13. Hannah had three children after William; two boys and one girl. His father remarried rather quickly and had four additional children beginning in 1854 by William's stepmother, Sarah.

William described his father as a "mover" who relocated 11 times between 1846 and 1858. Those locations remain unidentified. However, according to William's April 12, 1913, letter to the US Commissioner of Pensions quoted in Chapter X, they were all within the northeast US. In 1858, the John C. McLean family was living in Herkimer County, NY, and William was attending Fairfield Academy which was a large co-educational school in Fairfield. When the family decided to move to the area of Painesville, OH, a short time later, William may have originally moved with them or he elected to remain at Fairfield Academy to continue his education. According to the 1860 Federal Census, William was living with the Palmer Root family near Poland, NY. Poland was about 11 miles northwest of Fairfield. However, the 1861 catalogue for Fairfield Seminary shows William's residence as Painesville, OH.

During the school term William probably lived at the Academy. It is from Fairfield Academy that William enrolled in the 34th New York Infantry (Herkimer Regiment) on April 20, 1861. In one of his letters he says he "studied and taught till Sumpter (sic) fell". At the time of William's first pension application in 1879, he states that he was a farmer and a teacher when he enrolled. He was 21 years old and about the average size for the time. He stood 5'7" with black hair, hazel eyes, and a dark complexion.

Fort Sumter had fallen just a week earlier and Lincoln called for 75,000 volunteers to quell the rebellion. Surely, several factors entered into William's decision to enlist. Many of his fellow students, teachers, and friends from Fairfield and the surrounding towns enlisted at the same time. The state bounty may have provided encouragement as would the talk of a short-lived conflict. Evidence in his diary suggests that William may also have been a member of the Wide Awakes, a loose organization of young men who supported the Republican Party and campaigned for Lincoln's election in 1860. William's support of the Wide Awake movement may have influenced his decision to enlist.

William left from Herkimer with many of the other local enlistees to travel to Albany by rail where they were mustered into the Federal service on June 15, 1861. Although evidence shows that some in the regiment were reluctant to complete the mustering process, all were eventually enrolled for a period of two years. They were all Federal soldiers now. While in Albany, they viewed the body of Colonel Elmer Ellsworth who was killed in Alexandria, VA, on May 24th. The young men of the 34th certainly knew of Ellsworth's Fire Zouaves regiment and their reputation for precision military demonstrations and drills. For the first time, the men of the 34th realized the seriousness of the war. From Albany, the 34th joined several other New York regiments which were traveling to Washington City (now Washington, DC). They traveled by foot, rail, and water and arrived in a city teeming with new volunteers from several northern states. The vastness of the Washington with its statues, monuments and large government buildings impressed the many thousands of newly arrived soldiers.

For those readers unfamiliar with the usual size of Civil War military units, normally 100 men were assigned to a company upon enlistment. Ten companies generally constituted a regiment. There were exceptions to these numbers. During the war, with attrition and new recruits to fill depleted ranks, the total number of men who served in a particular regiment could be well over a thousand. As a new regiment formed at the very beginning of the war, the

34th New York was somewhat shy of these usual company and regiment totals.

For the next several months, the 34th was in two different camps within Washington City. Later they relocated to the upper Potomac River area and Camp Jackson for patrol duty along a 16 mile stretch of the river. Here they drilled, patrolled, foraged, and became accustomed to military routine. During August and September, William was treated for chronic diarrhea and missed several rotations of guard duty. It was in this area that a portion of the 34th, which did not include William, had its first minor engagement with the enemy. William relates this episode in his diary. This first diary ends on Saturday, October 5, 1861.

Later in the month, the regiment moved to Edwards Ferry in support of the units engaged at Ball's Bluff on October 21, 1861. Following this debacle, they went into winter camp at Poolesville, MD. In the late winter, they moved to Harper's Ferry and Bolivar, VA, (now West Virginia), before being assigned with the troops moving into southeastern Virginia for the Peninsula Campaign. The 34th saw action at Fair Oaks on May 31, 1862. This first action for the entire regiment saw 31 killed and 58 wounded, including three killed and six wounded from Company C, William's company.

The next action for the 34th was the Seven Days battles beginning on June 30th. They were engaged at White Oak Swamp where they had six killed and 11 wounded, although none were from Company C. On the following day the 34th was engaged at Malvern Hill, suffering two killed, Major Charles Brown and Sergeant George Morse. Through both of these actions William was present and came through unscathed.

The Herkimer Regiment retreated down the Peninsula with the rest of General George McClellan's troops and evacuated from the region along with the rest of the Federal troops. They eventually halted at Newport News, VA, where they remained until August 25. They then boarded a steamer for transport to Alexandria, VA. There was to be no rest for the regiment as news was received that Robert E. Lee had invaded Maryland and the regiment was needed to help quell the invasion. Marching through Washington City and near their old camp at Tenallytown, they proceeded northwest through Rockville, MD, and arrived at Keedsyville, MD, a few short miles from Sharpsburg, on September 15.

They lay in camp at Keedysville until the morning of September 17 when they received their marching orders. They tramped west, crossing Antietam Creek and through the North Woods. The regiment proceeded through the fields on the north side of the Smoketown Road and engaged the enemy from that point to just west of the Dunker Church. The unit became detached from its battle line and took heavy fire while inflicting the same on the Confederate troops before disengaging and retiring from the field. This action produced the regiment's largest number of casualties to date; 43 killed outright or mortally wounded and 74 wounded. Killed from Company C was William's friend, William A. Salisbury. Another close friend Charles A. Willoughby was wounded. Company C experienced four deaths and 11 wounded. Again William McLean emerged unscathed physically but the mental wounds were all too real.

On September 22, William and the regiment left the Sharpsburg area and proceeded to the Harper's Ferry area where they remained for more than a month before again heading to Virginia. This time the destination was Falmouth, across the Rappahannock River from Fredericksburg. Here they remained until 9:00 am on Saturday, December 13, when they crossed the river into Fredericksburg. They remained in town observing the battle until the afternoon when they were put in on the Federal right. Although not as heavily engaged as those troops storming the heights, the 34th nonetheless took substantial fire until the battle died down just after dark. The regiment was relieved from the field about midnight. This day the regiment suffered six killed and 11 wounded, one of those being William McLean. His luck had run its course.

William tells of his severe and painful wounding to his left foot with the loss of a toe. His wounding occurred about 5:00 pm on Saturday evening. He was evacuated across the river and later transferred to a boat going to the hospital at Point Lookout, MD. Point Lookout was also the location of a Federal prison camp for Confederate soldiers. Due to a bureaucratic mix-up while there, William was transferred with a group of Pennsylvania troops to Turner's Lane Hospital in Philadelphia, PA. He very much wanted to leave Point Lookout as his version of the story has him insisting that he be allowed to leave with the Pennsylvania troops. This decision later resulted in his being unaccounted for and listed as a deserter for several months. The company muster roll lists him as "deserted from the US service March 13, 1863". William was later transferred to a convalescent hospital near Alexandria, VA, from which he was returned to his unit on June 9, 1863. From that point on his service was uneventful. William J. McLean was mustered out with his regiment at Albany, NY, on June 30, 1863, which was the expiration of his term of service. Eleven hundred ten men had been mustered in on June 15, 1861, or later recruited. Those mustered out on June 30 totaled 496. The attrition rate for their length of service was 45%.

William returned from Albany to Little Falls with his regiment. A huge celebration was planned in the city park in the center of town. Little Falls was selected because it was the largest community in Herkimer County. A County Reception Committee was formed to plan the day-long events. Saturday, June 13, was the day designated for the welcoming party. Picnic tables and a platform for the orators were constructed. Decorations were ordered and hung. "In Ward's Square (the village's eastern park), long picnic tables were set up, store fronts and homes were decorated with banners and wreaths, and on Ann Street a large wooden monument had been erected in memory of the 34th's dead."

The monument, which was contributed by the Village of Little Falls, featured a 20 foot high shaft topped by a large eagle grasping an American flag in each talon. The column itself was wreathed with cedar boughs and white flowers and bore the names of the regiment's battles: Fair Oaks, Glendale, Antietam, Yorktown, Fredericksburg, South Mountain, Malvern Hill, Edwards Ferry, Nelson's Farm, Savage's Station, and Peach Orchard Station." The engagements were not listed in order since Edwards Ferry was their initial engagement and South Mountain was followed a few days later by Antietam. Nonetheless, the listing of their battle honors was impressive!

The 34th arrived in the Little Falls train depot at 11:00 a.m. By that time, the town was packed with welcomers who had been arriving since the announcement of the celebration. Folks had come from far and wide in carriages, wagons, horseback, and on foot. Several special trains had also arrived before the 34th at the depot. According to the local newspaper, the crowd was estimated at 10,000.

An invocation, welcoming addresses, and a parade preceded the arrival of the 34th at Ward's Square where a welcoming tribute was recited by 34 young ladies dressed in white. They stood on an elevated platform and were arranged in a "pyramid of beauty". Next, the hour-long main oration of the day was given by a local judge. Finally, the no-doubt hungry men were ushered to a thousand-foot-long table where they stuffed themselves to their heart's content while being waited on by over one hundred ladies of the town. Only after the soldiers had their fill was the general populace permitted time at the table. By 5:00 p.m. festivities of the day were over. Locals, who had mingled with the soldiers, gradually dispersed. Soldiers who were furloughed at Little Falls went on their way while others mounted the cars to take them back to Albany where they were to await their mustering out on June 30, 1863. It may be that William McLean was one of those on furlough and allowed to remain at home for a few days. However, those on furlough had to return to Albany at their own expense to be mustered out.[1]

Little Falls was on the regular rail route to Albany. Less than two years later, special railroad "cars" would again pass through both Little Falls and Herkimer on their way to Albany. This time the cars carried martyred President Abraham Lincoln from Washington City to his final resting place in Springfield, IL. At 7:35 on the evening of April 26, 1865, the six car special train passed through Little Falls. A large wreath consisting of a shield and cross welcomed the slow-moving train. The train did not stop. Fifteen minutes later, the train passed through Herkimer and was greeted by 36 women dressed all in white. Again the train could not pause but continued on to Albany where it would stop. It is not known if William McLean came to either location to observe the passing of the funeral train. It would be difficult to imagine that he did not.

---

1. The information in the preceding four paragraphs was excerpted from *Distant Drums, Herkimer County in the War of Rebellion*, David P. Krutz, pages 129-133.

John C. McLean, Private, Company F, 29th Ohio Infantry and Company K, 186th New York Infantry

John Carruthers McLean was the father of William and Simpson McLean. Both John and his son, Simpson, also served in the Civil War. William (21) was the first member of the family to enlist. William enlisted in early May, 1861, at Fairfield, NY where he was attending school and teaching. William probably had some influence over his father and his brother (Simpson) enlisting in the 29th Ohio later in the same year.

John was 44 at the time of his enlistment (45 being the maximum acceptable age for service). He was tending a farm of unknown acreage near Painesville, OH. According to William, his father moved to Mentor (Painesville post office) OH, in February, 1859. According to the Ancestry.com records John was born in Ayrshire, Scotland on February 13, 1815. However, some census records show John born in Ireland. His emigration date to the United States was likely 1839. This date is based on a census record for Simpson McLean from 1910 which noted his father's date of emigration. It is known that William was born in Philadelphia in 1840 at which time John would have been 23 years old. In a 1913 letter, William states that his father lived in the country on a farm prior to moving to Philadelphia City. John was not a big man, standing 5' 5-1/2' tall with a dark complexion, blue eyes, and brown hair as noted on his mustering information. He mustered in on September 18, 1861, for a term of service of three years as a private in Company F of the 29th Ohio Infantry, known as the "Giddings Regiment". The regiment was so named as it was organized by the noted Ohio abolitionist statesman, Joshua Reed Giddings.

The 1860 Federal census, recorded on June 16, 1860, reveals some interesting things about the John C. McLean family. They had five children at home. John stated that he worked as a day laborer. John enlisted six weeks before his son, Simpson. When John enlisted in September, 1861, he left the five children at home with his second wife, Sarah. Six weeks later his son, Simpson (16), enlisted. Now his wife Sarah was left at home with James (8), Caroline (6), and Henry (1). We are left to wonder how Sarah and the children survived on their farm with the two men of the house gone off to war. It is probable that the men leaving the household caused some degree of strife. But perhaps the payment of bounties was reason enough to permit the men to enlist. The bounties and the military pay could sustain the family for some time.

John mustered in at Camp Giddings near Jefferson, OH. Thus, he initially remained near his home as he trained and became accustomed to military life. He remained at Camp Giddings for a little more than three months and on Christmas Day, 1861, the regiment relocated to Camp Chase, four miles west of downtown Columbus, OH, where they continued to train. The regiment was a model in behavior and manners as the Ashtabula Sentinel wrote the following about the departure of the regiment on January 1, 1862.

> The regiment which left us last week was composed of farmers and mechanics from Summit, Medina, Trumball, and Ashtabula counties. They are temperate, industrious and intelligent. In their morals they represent the Western Reserve. During the time they have been with us we have seen no drunkenness, no broils, or fighting among them. No depredations have been committed upon the property of our citizens. They have been constant attendants upon our churches, have attended our social parties, and sat at our fire-sides. Officers and soldiers have been kind and gentlemanly in their deportment, and have made friends of our citizens, all of whom felt regret at the separation.

Less than a month later, on January 17, 1862, the regiment moved with other regiments to Cumberland, MD, after being assigned to the Army of the Potomac in the Third Brigade, Lander's Division. Here they were on guard duty at Hampton Heights and the Paw Paw Tunnel until March, 1862. The tunnel is a 3,118 foot long canal tunnel on the Chesapeake and Ohio Canal in Allegany County, MD. The regiment advanced on Winchester and Strasburg, VA, in early March and was engaged at the Battle of Winchester, March 22 and 23. No records remain of John's service during this time except that he was listed as present with the regiment. However by April 23, 1862, John is recorded as being "sick" and hospitalized at Mount Jackson, VA. The regiment was marching up the

Shenandoah Valley as it proceeded towards Fredericksburg, VA. It is unknown when John rejoined his regiment but he is listed as "present" again beginning in May.

The 29th Ohio was in the thick of the action at the Battle of Port Republic on June 9th and again two months later at the Battle of Cedar Mountain on August 9th in which John McLean was wounded. The nature and extent of his wound is not stated in the extant records. The hardships of military life, however, did not prove agreeable to John's constitution. Records show him being sick in a hospital at Alexandria, VA, for September and October, 1862. At some point John was moved to the Harewood Hospital near the Soldiers Home in Washington City. He was discharged from this hospital on November 14, 1862. The surgeon's report states John is afflicted with "chronic rheumatism affecting the joints and tissue of the heart increasing its action and accompanied with constant pain and general debility rendering him totally unfit for military service." He was granted one half disability and discharged. John returned to his home and farm in Ohio while his son, Simpson, continued his service in the 29th Ohio.

Harewood Hospital, circa 1864 (Source: Google Images).

Corporal Simpson McLean, Company F, 29th Ohio Infantry

When measured against his brother, William, and his father, John, Simpson McLean, William's younger brother, had the most interesting war and post-war history. Simpson rose higher in the ranks, served longer, was in a greater number of battles and engagements, was wounded three times, and had a more successful postwar life than either William or John. This was in spite of the fact that Simpson began his service with a lie which went undiscovered.

Simpson McLean was born March 1, 1845, in or near Philadelphia, PA. Several documents and census records show Simpson born in Ireland, from where his parents emigrated; but this may not be correct. William, Simpson's older brother, was born in Philadelphia in 1840 so it is unlikely that his parents were back in Ireland five years later. The family emigrated sometime in 1839 (per the 1910 Federal census for Simpson McLean) and settled near Philadelphia where John was a farmer. Twenty years later, in February, 1859, according to his son, William, the family moved to near Painesville, OH. Previously, they had been living in Herkimer County, NY, for some years. Simpson moved to Ohio with the family while his brother, William, remained in Herkimer County to continue his education.

When the war broke out in April, 1861, Simpson had just turned 16 years old. Simpson and his father were interested in enlisting. It may have been through the influence of William and his letters or perhaps the bounty amounts that would help sustain the family that solidified their decision. Simpson enlisted and mustered into Captain Morse's Company of the 29th Ohio Infantry on November 1, 1861. His father had mustered in six weeks earlier. Simpson was exactly 16 years and eight months old. He is carried on the muster roles as being 18. Thus the lie, which was not uncommon, was fabricated to allow him to serve in the same company as his father. This company became Company F of the 29th Ohio. His term of service was for three years. The preceding short biography for John McLean provides additional information on the family at the time of Simpson's enlistment. Simpson was somewhat small for his age, standing just 5 feet, 4-1/2 inches tall with a light complexion, gray eyes, and dark brown hair. Although his weight is not provided, he was probably about 130-140#. Carrying a musket and full complement of accoutrements, which could easily weigh 40 pounds or more, would provide a challenge for Simpson.

Private Simpson McLean initially trained at Camp Giddings near Jefferson, OH. Three months later the regiment relocated to Camp Chase, four miles west of downtown Columbus. By the early spring 1862 the regiment was in the Shenandoah Valley of Virginia. Their first significant combat was in the Battle of Kernstown, VA, on March 23, 1862. Kernstown is just a few miles south of Winchester which had been a Confederate stronghold early in the war. Sunday was a day usually to be avoided for battles; but not on this day. The 29th had been depleted from its initial strength of about a thousand men by disease, resignations, and a few desertions. Today, the 716 remaining soldiers and officers were to have their resolve tested. Also, until this day, few of the Giddings Boys had experience in firing their rifled muskets. On passing through Winchester they stopped to load and cap their muskets in preparation for what was to come. They kept their muskets loaded until late in the afternoon. It was 4:00 p.m. before they were finally thrust into the fray. The 29th was in hot fire for several hours until darkness came and the field was left to the dead, dying, and wounded. Simpson McLean, however, emerged unscathed.

Like so many other new soldiers beginning a life with hundreds of other men from different areas and environments, disease was bound to be an issue. Accordingly, Simpson found himself in the regimental hospital in Mount Jackson, VA, beginning April 23, 1862. He rejoined his regiment and was present for the Battle of Port Republic on June 9th. Again, Simpson was untouched. The regiment remained in Virginia and had a respite from conflict for several months. Their next engagement was at Cedar Mountain on August 9th. This encounter proved fateful for the McLeans of the 29th Ohio. Both Simpson and his father were wounded in this battle. Simpson was slightly wounded in the leg and the wound proved of no consequence. The nature and extent of John's wound is not contained in the official records but John McLean was to be discharged from the service a few months later. The balance of 1862 was uneventful for the 29th.

In March, 1863, Simpson received a promotion to Corporal. The records do not indicate how he happened to come by this promotion nor do they indicate if he was elected by his company or appointed. The promotion resulted in additional pay for Simpson and his family. In any event, he was able to gain a few short months experience before the unit's next engagement. The 29th Ohio was engaged at the horrific Battle of Chancellorsville on May 1-3, 1863. The unit went into battle severely understrength with about 500 men. They saw their greatest action in the area just south of Chancellor's Crossroads. By virtue of their location, they experienced the waning effects of Stonewall Jackson's charge after he made the famous flank march. The following day, May 3, they were subject to heavy action from artillery and infantry for many hours before being forced to retire from the field. During this time they made several charges against the enemy. They were one of the last, if not the last, regiment to evacuate from the area. As they evacuated they saw the burning Chancellorsville Inn with rebel troops gathered around it. The 29th lost over 70 men; 24 killed, 42 wounded, and 28 taken prisoner including some who were wounded. Simpson emerged without a scratch.

The regiment, which at this time was attached to the Army of the Potomac and Slocum's Twelfth Corps, Candy's Brigade, left Virginia and crossed over into Maryland at Edwards Ferry on June 26th. A few months later, Simpson's brother, William, was at Edwards Ferry on October 21-23, 1861, during the Ball's Bluff debacle. Simpson's regiment, camped near the Monocacy Bridge, made their way along the C&O Canal and arrived in Frederick, MD, on June 29th. From Frederick they marched northeast, through Taneytown, MD, and soon entered southern Pennsylvania. Here they were to gain fame on the morning of July 3, 1863, on the southeastern slope of Culp's Hill. By nightfall of June 30th, they were at Littlestown, PA, ten miles southwest of Gettysburg. After resuming their march in the morning and resting at Two Taverns, halfway to Gettysburg, they became aware of the conflict raging ahead and were hurried the final few miles. They camped for the night a couple hundred yards to the left of the Baltimore Pike and near two prominent round-topped hills, one higher than the other. These hills had no local names at this time but are now readily known to Civil War readers. Their assignment, on the morning of July 2nd, was defense of the ground just north of these Round Tops and along the southern contours of Culp's Hill. Although not involved, they were well aware of the fighting to their left in places like the Peach Orchard, Devil's Den, and Little Round Top. An excellent accounting of the 29th at Culp's Hill is contained in *The Untried Life, the 29th Ohio Volunteer Infantry in the Civil War* (2012) by James T. Fritsch.

Sometime during their day long engagement on Culp's Hill, Simpson McLean experienced his most grievous wound of the three he was to endure during the war. He was struck by a minie ball in the right thigh. The ball entered 7" above the patella (kneecap) in the center of the thigh, partially splintered the femur as it passed downward, and exited 3" above the knee. This was a significantly disabling wound. It is not recorded as to what occurred after McLean was struck but he was not captured and he was taken to a field hospital. This is the type of wound which would normally result in an amputation well above the wound. In Simpson's case, amputation never occurred. Records indicate he was to remain in Gettysburg at the hospital for about 16 days before being transported to an Army hospital at Annapolis, MD. Simpson was perhaps a patient at Camp Letterman for a short while as this large hospital was begun on July 5th. He was to remain at the Annapolis hospital for 6 months.

One can only imagine the suffering Simpson had to endure during this lengthy recuperation. As was customary for recovering soldiers at that time, he received a month's furlough on February 5, 1864. Simpson certainly traveled home to Ohio to be united with his father and the rest of his family. He was briefly readmitted to the hospital at Annapolis after returning on March 3 so he could be examined prior to returning to his unit. His recovery was reasonably complete as he was not discharged but cleared to return to his regiment on March 8.

A sister regiment to the 29th Ohio was the 7th Ohio Infantry. Reenlistment problems in the 7th caused several men and officers from the 29th to be temporarily transferred to that regiment. Muster Roll records indicate that Corporal McLean was transferred to Company G of the 7th from December 22, 1863, to March 22, 1864; however he may never have reported to the regiment since he was still hospitalized and on furlough. The company muster roll for

Company G of the 7th OH for January and February, 1864, shows Simpson as absent and in the hospital due to his wound. Apparently this was just a paper transfer. Simpson is shown as present with the 29th OH for March and April, 1864, where he continued to serve until discharged.

While Simpson was recovering from his severe Gettysburg wound and absent from his regiment, the regiment was transferred to the Department and Army of Ohio and Cumberland. They were now part of the western theater of operations. Simpson was slightly wounded for the third and final time below the right knee at Stone Mountain, GA, on June 16, 1864. It does not appear that he lost any time due to this wound. He was to remain with his unit until discharged in Atlanta at the expiration of his three-year term of service on November 1, 1864. He was provided transportation by the military as far as Cleveland, OH. From there he was on his own to make the final 30 miles to his home in the vicinity of Painesville. Simpson was 19 years old and a hardened veteran of 19 battles over three years. He endured three wounds and saw multiple friends killed, seriously wounded, and struck down by disease. But yet his life was just beginning.

Chapter III

Antebellum Herkimer County, Fairfield, and Fairfield Seminary (Academy)

Herkimer County is an odd-shaped elongated county in upstate New York, approximately 70 miles west of Albany. Today, the New York State Thruway passes through the southern portion of the county. In the very early years, the main transportation route through Herkimer County was the Erie Canal, opened in 1825, which passed through Utica and Little Falls. While today's population of this largely rural county is just over 62,000; in 1860 it was only a small percentage of that number. The county had been in existence since 1791 and its present boundaries were established in 1817. When white settlers first came into the area in the early 1720s, they competed for land with the native Mohawk Indians, members of the Iroquois Confederacy. As was normal for the time, settlers and the Indians did not always co-exist amicably and several atrocities permeate the early history of the area.

The settlers were not about to leave, however, and they established communities and villages near sources of waterpower and in the fertile hill country. Wheat farming was eventually supplanted by dairy farming and by the 1850s Little Falls was known for its cheese production. In addition to the canal, railroads provided transportation for local goods to reach the markets at Albany and beyond. Towns and villages sprang up in close proximity to these transportation avenues. Many of these were small crossroad communities consisting of a few residences and small businesses to service their needs. In some respects, not much has changed since 1860.

Remington Arms Company, founded in 1816, located in Illion, NY, close to the Erie Canal, Mohawk River, and the railroad, quickly became the major industry of the county and the region. German and Irish immigrants, seeking a better life for themselves and their families, provided a ready source of labor. Remington Arms became a major supplier of small arms to the US military before and during the Civil War, second only to Colt. In fact, Remington revolvers were presented to the 34th New York Infantry as they left Herkimer County for their mustering in at Albany in May, 1861.

On the eve of the Civil War, Herkimer County remained mostly rural with small farms and towns dotted throughout the populated southern portion of the county. These were hard working immigrants and citizens who had moved west from other areas of the New York state and the northeast. As the population increased, schools were established to educate the youth. One such school was established at the Town of Fairfield, located seven miles north of Little Falls and eleven miles from Herkimer. This area was settled as early as 1785 as a German settlement. The area around Fairfield grew slowly but by 1802 Fairfield Academy was established as a school for men. A charter was granted in 1803 by the New York State Board of Regents. In 1812 the Trinity Episcopal Church in Fairfield sought to establish a college of "liberal culture" under Episcopal auspices. This did not occur and the following year Trinity Church founded a theological college in association with the Academy and Seminary. This association continued for a few years until the academy was reorganized as the co-educational Fairfield Seminary in 1839, incorporating as a "Classical Academy and Female Collegiate Institute." It had both a teacher training program and a college preparation curriculum. From its early years the academy had several instructors schooled in medical subjects such that by 1812 the academy applied for a charter as a medical college so it could grant medical degrees to its graduates. The charter was granted and this portion of the institution became known as the Fairfield Medical College. The medical college had as many as 200 medical students at one time and granted over 600 medical degrees during its 28 years of existence. The medical college continued until 1840 when competition within and outside of New York state forced its closing.

At the time of his military enlistment, William McLean was both a student and a teacher at Fairfield Seminary. In the spring of 1861, Fairfield Seminary was a prosperous high school and college preparatory institution with an enrollment of 551 scattered over "five large and commodious buildings" which included dormitories. The 1861 catalogue noted that "The Gentlemen's rooms are fifteen by eighteen feet, and each for only two occupants. The 'Ladies' Building' is a fine new edifice, one hundred and twenty feet in length, and three stories high. It is entirely *separate* from those of the Gentlemen, and has a large and pleasant GYMNASIUM, appropriately furnished. Ladies have access to the Dining Hall and Chapel without going out of doors. The Principal, Preceptress, and nearly all the faculty, board in the Hall with the students."[2] The three and four story brick buildings were situated on several acres in a park-like setting at the main crossroads of the town. Both a three-year and a five-year course of study were offered. "*Constant and assiduous attention* is given to those branches essential to a thorough education, and it is the *highest ambition* of the Institution to prepare young men for college, business or a profession." Each year consisted of three terms, beginning with the Fall Term in August, the Winter Term in early December, and the Summer Term beginning in March and ending in early July. The catalogue further noted that Fairfield had three churches; Methodist, Episcopalian, and Presbyterian. Students came from the northeast, the Middle Atlantic States, and even from the south to attend Fairfield Seminary. Their circular proclaimed easy access from all parts of the country but noted that folks would have to leave the railroad at Little Falls or Herkimer, from which transportation to the Seminary was free on the first day of each term. As new major transportation routes developed in the 19th century, bypassing the Town of Fairfield, the academy lost its prominence. It operated as a military academy beginning in 1891. Fairfield Academy closed in 1901, largely due to competition from the growing number of high schools in the area. Unfortunately, none of the buildings have survived.

2. *Catalogue of the Officers and Students of Fairfield Seminary, 1861.*

32   A Soldier's Life in the Civil War

FAIRFIELD SEMINARY, FAIRFIELD, N. Y.

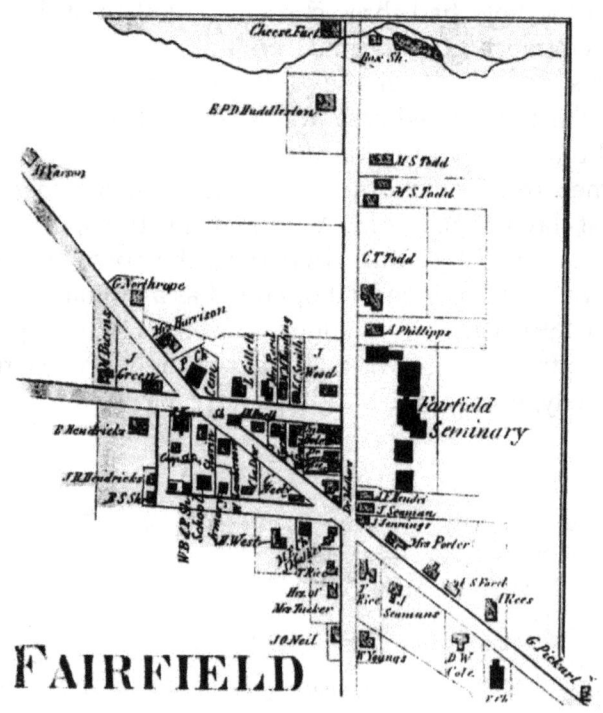

CHAPTER IV

May 1861: Enlistment and Mustering

May 1861

M^3 *6th* This is a rainy AM. I took my desk and bank to Mr. Northup's[4], he took a lot of us volunteers to Herkimer. We waited at Middleville[5] an hour and ½ for the company from Gray's[6] which came in great big & went on to H(erkimer). I got a revolver[7] presented to me at Fairfield. There was no rain on our journey. We had dinner at H(erkimer) then it rained and lasted all day. We took the cars at 4 ½ PM & had a pleasant ride to Albany. Then we had to lay in the rain from 8 til 10. Then we got our supper which was compose of perch, beef, water, mustard and salt. I never was in so noisy a place. Then we were marched to the church, well soked in rain water, to take our bed in a soft pine floor with a straw mattress and one blanket, with our boots for a pillow. The captain[8] shared part of my bed which was small.

3. McLean's day of the week abbreviation for Monday; follows throughout the diary for all days of the week.
4. This may be George Northup (47) a laborer in Fairfield with whom William may have boarded. An Emerson S. Northup (19) lived 5 miles away in Salisbury and may have been a fellow student at Fairfield Academy. Emerson enlisted May 1 at Salisbury and was mustered into Company K as 1st Lieutenant.
5. Middleville is 3 miles west of Fairfield.
6. Town of Gray is 10 miles north of Fairfield; also known as Grays and Graysville.
7. Most likely a Remington .44 cal revolver from the nearby Ilion, NY factory.
8. The Captain of Company C was Thomas Corcoran (23) of Graysville (town name as used in the regimental history).

Captain Thomas Corcoran, date unknown. (Source: American Civil War Database.)

T 7th I got up feeling well, after washing and wiping with our pocket handkerchiefs. We were marched to brf (breakfast) through the streets. At the house we had to wait a long time for our turn. At last we got the same food as before except coffee. We were taken back then were excused. I had a pass and fellows in my care. We went to the _____ on a ferry and back again. Then got dinner as before. Then I was excused to rove again. All one could see was volunteers. We crossed the ferry again. At last night came we had the same supper but I did not eat. I went with some of the boys to the Theator and called at the saloon to get oysters = .38 and .15 to go in the theator. It was the first that ever I was in and I saw enough (of Bablon). I got back at 12 oclock to loging and there was so much noise in building as in a mad house. I _____ bed down and tried to sleep but was soon hailed by one who said I had his bunk. We lay together-noise was kept up. But we soon was in the land of dreams.

W 8 We were marched up to the Capital and entered the front yard went through stand, then came back. I had a pain in my stomach and had to wait an hour at the Adams House[9] in the street for breakfast (we did ditto). I went to the river and shot my pistle a

9. The 34th was first quartered in the old Adams House in the heart of the city. The 1903 regimental history refers to the Adams House as an "old rat hole" with "utter disregard of sanitary laws."

number of times and made good shots. We held an election of offeciers. I run for 2nd Corporl but was defeated. We went to diner (oh dito). I then went with Mr. Banks[10] till my feet ached. Then we run some balls and returned. This is play and we had pay for it. I wrote some xc.[11] After tea I went with some of V til 10. I had soor feet and was tired. Noise. Noise. All is bustle and noise.

Th 9th Aft(er) br(eakfast) I and 2 others went over the river & went out into the country to shoot our pistles and had sport. I was told at dinner that there were eaten in one day at the Adams House 2,783 loaves of bread by the vol. I run some balls. I went through the streets in the PM with (undetermined name) till 10. I slept coldly.

F 10th I can sleep in the noise and tumult of talk, walking, xc as well as in silence. We were exam today, striped[12] I did not like my din(ner). So I went with Amos Morse[13] to a Sallan (saloon) & had oysters. I then came and wrote a letter to Benie[14] and mailed it +.125.[15] I went to the post office. I got .50 for examining 2 heads which I did afterward. There were 3 drunk in the building and they did get crasy. They took (undetermined words).

S 11th This is a wet day. I went to the museum. I saw all Birds, animals, fishes, snakes, shells, stones all _____. Looked till my eyes were tired. So ends the week.

Sab(bath) 12th I went to the Roman Church. I cannot describe the beauty of it. I never saw the like before. I wrote some and went to the Methodist church at n(ight). We had an extry sermon, but I was too warm and sleepy.

M 13th I sent letters to Miss R Northrup,[16] Miss M J Gardiner[17,]

10. Harrison L. Banks (20) enlisted May 1 at Fairfield, mustered in as a Corporal in Co. C.
11. McLean's abbreviation for etcetera.
12. This was their military physical examination.
13. Amos Morse (20) enlisted May 1 at Graysville as a private in Co. C.
14. Bernie Hines
15. In 1860 the postage rate was .03 per ½ ounce for travel up to 3,000 miles. This may represent .125 cents.
16. The 1860 census shows a Rosina Northup (21) residing in Fairfield with her father, 47-year old George, and Anna (33), Sarah (12), and Albert (3).
17. Margaret J. Gardner would become William McLean's wife December 30, 1863, after his discharge from the 34th. The 1860 census shows Margaret Gardner (18) living near Frankfort in Herkimer County with her father and four siblings.

& father. I went to the Museum and wrote some there. I feel bad in my bowels. I bought salts and took them then I lay round til n(ight).

T 14th   I examined R Mannings[18] head[19], and was on gard all day. The day was rainy. I came on gard 2 hours at 11 ½. It was a sleepy time.

W 15   I wrote a letter to Uncle John. We m[arched] some in the streets xc. I went to the river and in the aft[ernoon]. There was a flag raised at the post office. I never saw such a crowd.

Th 16th   This is a warm d(ay). We m(arched) to the capital and parted into squads. Burt[20] took our sq(uad) to the river and m(arched) there ½ mile. Then we lay round I rote a let(ter) to G. Carpinter[21]. I got one from Miss R. Northrup. Some of us went to meeting. I never was so courtiously entertained. There were 3 ladys that shook hands with us and sang for us xc.

F 17th   I did not eat my breakfast, it was so bad. We were almost going to tip it out the window. I put a dish of slop under the table and coffee xc. Then I went to the river; went on a steemer and all over and through it. Bought aples at 8 cts each. A lady gave me a paper of fried cakes for the company to devide with. We had a good dinner than marched to the capital from there. I went to the country and pass over 4 miles. We saw some nice things, trees in bloom ripe with tomatos xc. We went over fences xc. I came to the store and wrote on the corner. I went to the 4th Presbyterian Church. They had a prayer meeting and preacher called on the bretheran to pray. They stood up. I was welcomed through not interested[22].

S 18th   I went with company to the capt., then I went to the warfe and waited 4 hrs to see a regiment of V(olunteers) go to NY. O what a crowd in the boats, house tops, xc. 4 of the V fell overboard. One of them jumped over and did not want to get back. It was a busy time. Some guns were fired. One regiment came from Gray on a bard (barge) towed by a steamer. They cut loose below (undetermined words). I went to (line erased).

18. Richard Manning (21), Co C enrolled May 1 at Poland, NY.
19. Possible reference to examining for lice.
20. William S Burt (29), Co C enrolled May 1 at Graysville.
21. Gertrude Carpenter of Norway, 19 years old in 1860. She was a student at Fairfield Seminary in 1861.
22. McLean makes a heavy cross in pencil here; the significance of which remains unexplained.

May 1861   39

Sab 19th I went to the ME Ch (Methodist Episcopal Church) in the AM. I went to Tweedle (sic) Hall to metting PM. There was a crowded house & good sermon. This is cold spring uncommonly so. I went to meeting at the Bpst(Baptist) Tabernacle tonight.

[*Editor's Note.* Tweddle Hall served primarily as a lecture and music hall in its upper-level great hall while housing offices and stores on the lower of its four levels. The venue was named after Mr. John Tweddle. Tweddle worked as a well-known supplier of malt grains to breweries in addition to serving as president of Merchants Bank for over two decades. The prominent corner of State and Pearl Streets, widely known for the well-aged and enormous elm tree at its center, hosted the building. Tweddle purchased the property and its original structure in 1857, but chose to have a new stone building erected beginning in 1859 and in a more refined style. The four-story free-stone building had a frontage of 88 feet on State Street and 116 feet on North Pearl Street. The building cost $100,000 and was opened on June 28, 1860, filling a tremendous need for a public hall in the capital city. It soon hosted musical performances, temperance rallies, political meetings, conventions, and relief fund events. The hall hosted such notables of the times Perepa Rosa, Ristori, Dickens, Forrest, Edwin Booth and others. Unfortunately, the building burned on January 16, 1883 at a loss of $300,000.]

M 20th This is a cool AM. I wrote a letter to Andy Young and slept some. I marched P.M. At (undetermined word) I went to the warfe and called at the post office. (Next 3 lines are erased but 2 of the lines contain a bold + at the end of the line.)

T 21st I came to the church and wrote some. This is a warm day. I did not drill. I never felt better. I got a letter from father[23] and uncle John[24]. I took 2 shirts to have washed then came home and bunked.

W 22 I wrote a let to Simpson[25] and got one from Benie. P.M. we M(arched) to the river and crossed the ferry then went in swiming. The water was cold but healthy. At n(ight) there was a fire at

---

23. John C. McLean (44) enlisted as a Private in Co F, 29th Ohio Infantry September 18, 1861.
24. Uncle John remains unidentified further.
25. Simpson McLean (16) brother of William, later enlisted in Co F, 29th Ohio November 1, 1861.

Tweddle Hall, circa 1876 (Source: Wikipedia).

Tweddle Hall Assembly Area (Source: Library of Congress).

the brewery. It began at 6 and was put out at 9. The uper story was badly burned. O what a crowd. I come back and bunked.

Th 23 I was on gard. I did not sleep much. I went to meeting. It was a time of refreshing.

F 24th I got my name cut on my revolver = .25. I bought 3 coats and a pair of pants all = 5.00 I went to the corner of State St and got my washing. We marched to the fery and crossed over. The dust blew awfuly. We jump some. I went to meeting after seeing a man walk a rope from the top of one house to another across the st(reet).

S 25 I wrote let(ter) to father AM; PM I marched up the R.R. track a mile, came to a pond and a lot of us went in the swim. Some of us rode back in a train of sand cars. We the(n) went to the canel. I saw the same place that I saw 10 years ago. It looked the same. I was on a boat in a lock I came to the depot and there was an ingine off of the track they had a time geting it on. We had a march after supper and music.

26 Sab I took a march up the (undetermined) R and got on a train and rode back. I then went to church P.M. I went with the company to Tweddle Hall and heard abolishment sermon. O what meetings we have, such crowds. The preacher spoke of the death of Colonel Elsworth (sic) who was assasinated at Alexandria, Va. I got a crew of boys to go to a meeting with me AM and heard a sermon.

[*Editor's Note*. Colonel Elmer Ellsworth was a friend of President Abraham Lincoln and in 1860 worked in his law office in Springfield, IL. In 1861 he accompanied Lincoln on his trip to Washington for the inauguration. Later Ellsworth recruited the 11th New York Volunteer Regiment (Fire Zouaves) from the ranks of the New York City volunteer firefighters. The trained them and became their colonel. On May 24, 1861 he led them into Alexandria, Virginia to remove a Confederate flag flying from the roof of the Marshall House. While coming down the interior stairs, James W. Jackson, the hotel owner, confronted Ellsworth and killed him with a shotgun blast. Jackson was then killed by Corporal Francis Brownell. Lincoln had his friend's body brought to the White House where he laid in state in the East Room before being transported to New York City and Albany. Ellsworth was buried in the Hudson View Cemetery in his hometown of Mechanicville, NY, 20 miles north of Albany. Colonel Elmer Ellsworth was later awarded the Medal of Honor].

M 27th We have some showers. Our company were marched through the Capital to see the corpse of the late Colonel Elsworth. O what a crowd. I never was so jamed. Some boys, women & even men were hurt. We m(arched) P.M. At noon there was no butter and there was some awful noise. We lay round P.M. and had some sport on (undetermined) in boys and puting them under gard for fun. I went to prayer meeting with a number of boys. I felt blest and accepted of God.

T 28th This is a very cold day. I felt cold in the bunk. One fellow took my blanket off but I caught him at it. We had a high time. After breakfast Mr Hays[26] went with me to the fary. There we set and read and wrote while the boats made a number of (undetermined). I went P.M. all over the west part of the city. There was a circus there. I saw 4 elephants. I got back and took a nap. Then I got a crew to go to the meeting with me.

W 29 Some rain PM. I went upon the cars 3 miles with Hays. They stoped and we came back across lots. I went to a meeting and heard Mr. Welsh[27] preach against popery. He showed the beeds & bones of saints xc.

Th 30 We m after breakfast. I had a nap. We formed in a rigment (regiment). PM

had good music. We then crossed the R(iver). Some played ball and some shot at a mark. I shot 14 times wildly. I went to meeting though my mind was deviating.

F 31 This is warm and pleasant A.M. We crossed the R went in to swim, then played ball[28]. PM I lay round. I m(arched) some at N(ight)in the Sts(streets)[29]. There was a fellow taken by the police and hurt some. I saw the mob. So ended the month of May.

26. Martin V. Hayes (22) enlisted in Co C at Graysville May 5, 1861.
27. Perhaps Patrick Welsh (19) who enlisted at Albany June 16th.
28. A likely reference to baseball.
29. At this point McLean inserts a small drawing of a girl in a dress and the bold cross seen earlier.

CHAPTER V

June 1861: Albany Experiences and Orders to Travel

June 1861

S. 1st. This is pleasant. We M some. I crossed the R. before the breakfast. I then packed my things. The camp the(n) M to the barax (barracks) it was along M. We were ready for dinner which was relished well. PM We were all presented with a Testament. My feet were sore from the long walk on the paved sts. We had our quarters high in the 4th story.[30] Oh what a place. At 9 the tattoo was sounded the canon was fired and for the first time since I came to Alb I found myself in a still place here. Orders must be obeyed and noise stoped at 9 ½ (9:30 pm). So ends the day. I received my blanket.

Sab 2nd At the sound of the Tattoo and canon we were sumoned up xc. After washing answering to this, we were called to bft at 7. I slept some PM. We were called to listen to a sermon which was delivered in the front yard to a crowd. We were called to a dress parade at 5. We did some pitching quoits, some jumping xc xc. O what a Sab.

M 3 This is a wet AM. We had 2 short drills one AM & PM with the dress parade at 5. I had the blues all day a(nd) catched a cold at night.

T 4th I have an awful headache. I lay down to sleep after the roll was called and slept till breakfast. I went out then to play ball and lay by the fence in the hot sun till N(oon). PM I lay on the grass till 3. I bathed my head then came to the quarters & lay down and wrote. I did not (go) to dress parade or supper.

30. This was when the regiment was moved to the "large Industrial School Barracks, in the suburbs of the city, where there was plenty of room, inside and out." noted in the regimental history.

W 5 I got up in time to go to brft. I could not swallow. I went to see the Dr. He gave me pills and put some acid in my throat. I (undetermined) for the first time in the rig though my head ached. I had milk for din(dinner). PM I slept till dress p(arade) I saw the Dr. After tea he gave me a powder. The fever increased. The day was very warm. I covered up a sweet (sweat) & took nothing.

Th 6 AM wet. I got a pass til 3 PM. I was treated to a beer. I all over the city and crossed the R. sts some. I was back for diner & drilled. PM at m(arch), more fever.

F 7th Warm. I wrote a let for Andrew Warner.[31] Sold pants for 1.25 to Greenly.[32] Took a bathe, washed shirt & drawers xc. M I felt like having sport xc I did so.

S 8th I was on gard all day, doing room duty sweeping xc. I drilled some.

Sab 9 I wrote some this (15 lines smudged and some unreadable; mentions going to preaching, a volunteer who was sunstruck, and sending 3 letters)

M 10th I sent 3 leters (A large portion of this entry is unreadable due to smearing of pencil writing.) I went to tea alone.

11th We were drilled before brft then round till dress p(arade). I got asleep and did not go to d(ress) p(arade).

W 12 We dr(illed) before brft. I went out on a pass PM. 5 of us went back into pine grove a played there a while. I had a bad headache and swolen throat. I did not go to supr.

Th 13 PD[33] All as usual.

F 14 P. D. I have a sore throat yet. Mr Van Patten[34] made us a visit. I got a let from Simpson AM. I drilled some.

S 15 We were called out at 9 & at 12 we were mustered into the U.S. service and sworen in.[35] Some of the boy(s) refused to take the oath they were taken to the guardhouse amidst grones and sneers.

31. Andrew Warner (31) Co. C, enlisted May 1 at Poland, NY.
32. Hiram E. Greenly (31) Co. K, enlisted May 1 at Salisbury, NY.
33. Here McLean begins using letter abbreviations of undetermined meaning.
34. Rev. John B. Van Petten (40) enrolled June 15 at Albany as regimental chaplain. He was also a professor at Fairfield Academy.
35. According to Colonel Suiter, 786 officers and men were sworn in on Saturday, June 15.

Some were (undetermined) pulled and picked xc by the enfuriated crowed of vol. As the Co's were sworn there was some loud cheering and tossing of hats. PM all those that went to the gr hous sworn in. We fooled round on drs p (undetermined).

[*Editor's Note.* At the muster in, June 15, an opportunity was given to any, who didn't like the prospect ahead, to back out; and there were some faint hearts, who availed themselves of the chance; but generally speaking there was little disposition to do this. The regiment was drawn up, and a company at a time held up the right hands and swore to support and defend the country. When any men in a company backed out, there was a universal howl from all the others in the regiment. And when any company stood solidly up, and took the oath to a man, there was a universal cheer. Most of the cases of backing out were due to misgivings which the men began to have about their pay; for some, we must remember, had already been in the service nearly two months, and as yet no pay had materialized. But usually, when reassured on this point, they stepped back into the ranks. (Excerpted from the regimental history)]

Sab 16th WD 35 of us went to a creek in file a distance of 3 miles to bathe with leiutenent Butler.[36] PM I wrote. Some of the boys pitched cents all D(ay). We had no preaching.

M 17 PD AM I drilled some but pitched some penies. PM a rigment went off to NY. Our reg was in line along the road. O how we cheered. I could not speak plain after it.

T 18 I drilled in the rig. We had some double quick time. PM I went into a pine tree
in the back yeard & saw another rig leave. All else the same.

W 19th I wrote some of a missionary discourse and drilled as usual +

Th 20th WD I am on poleice (police) duty. I swept all the AM. PM I piched cents again. Mr Hiram Grenley told me his love & courtship adventures. Very strange.

F 21st I had a pass and went to (the) city. I went to Canal St got beer and sacars (cigars) for 3 of us by guessing on the date of a cent. I crossed the R. I got envelopes = '15 likeness = 15. I saw a man put

---

36. Samuel P. Butler (26) enrolled May 1 at Fairfield, mustered in as 1st Lieutenant, Co. C June 15th.

in the watchhouse for fighting. He was beastly drunk and awfuly covered with blood. We were back at 4 PM. Some rain. A souave (Zouave) was shot[37] while drilling some of their boy. They knew not of the gun being loaded. He never moved.

S 22 WD I wrote some. Examined a head. Drilled as usual xc. I (got) a let from Miss M A Davis. I was put on guard at the officers room aft tea. I went into the back yeard with the waiters. They drilled some & gave me all the milk I could drink, cold and hot. I had a bul(l)y[38] time. I got 2 let, one from A. Willoughby and one from J. Leawton.

Sab 23 I wrote some 3 lets; one for A. Warner, one Ed Snyder,[39] and one to Simpson. Also one to Amelia Van Slyke of Manheim.[40] I heard a sermon in the yeard PM. Cool night.

M 24 I wrote a let to Nelson Carpenter[41] and Uncle John. We had tea for supper with milk or sugar. We don't like it the best. I examined heads.

T 25 WD AM I did not drill. I got a let from Beny and from Magie Gardiner. I answered Magies. I have a poor appetite. All goes well. I let Martin Zimerman[42] take my revolver and gave him my likeness. He was going home.

W 26 WD I examined six heads =1'50. Did not drill. PM we were called to sign our names to the payroll. We were marched into back yeard to get our money. As soon as the money began to pass round there was a heavy shower. We retreated to the barracks and got our doe. There was $16.20 to me.

Th 27 There was some gambling. Another regt went off. We cheered them as if they were only going to return again but (2 undetermined words). There were a number of our boys that went

---

37. The regimental history does not mention this event.
38. "Bully" was a word frequently used to denote a good or fun time.
39. Edwin Snyder (34) Co. C, enlisted May 1 at Norway.
40. The 1860 census lists Amelia Van Slyke of Manheim as 20 years old.
41. Nelson H. Carpenter of Norway was 49 years old in 1860 and the father of Gertrude Carpenter.
42. Martin Zimmerman (18) enlisted May 1, mustered into Co. B as a Musician; deserted September 21, 1861 at Seneca Mills, MD. At this time, he may have been furloughed.

home to visit, it being there last chance. Some of the boys had their fathers come and get them. I wrote some.

F 28 I had a pass till 8 oclock. I got my likeness taken shooting. J. D I let Murry[43] have mine. We had a high time. I bought a coat and sold it for '25 more. There were another regt going off. I saw them on board of the boat. There was a fellow of our Regt drunk in the city. He gave me $1.00 to take care of. I went with him till 8 oclock then he got away + from me on the sly.[44] I then came to the barracks. I was back at 9. O what a time we have had O O +.

S 29 WD H Greenly payed me for the pants he got = 1,25. I sent 15.00 & got gold for it at the bank. I sold 3 coats for 5,50. Our clothing came. We got our overcoats. They were a light blue.

Sab 30 I (wrote) 3 lets; one to father, one for Fetterly[45] & one for Bennett.[46] We got our roundabouts,[47] canteen, haversacks and napsks. I packed some of my things. The orders to m(arch) to Wsht (Washington City) was read at dress parade. So we leave tomorrow. We have not drilled for a week. I feel quite well. I got let from Magie G and one from N Carpenter. All goes well.

43. James Murry (19) enlisted May 1 at Fairfield, mustered into Co. C.
44. Again McLean adds a small drawing of a girl in a dress.
45. Auberly Fetterly (19) enlisted May 1 at Fairfield, mustered into Co. C
46. Ashel Bennett (19) and Benjamin F. Bennett (23) enlisted May 1 at Graysville and mustered into Co. C.
47. A short, single-breasted, button front uniform jacket.

CHAPTER VI

July 1861: Washington City and the Aftermath of Bull Run

July 1861

    M 1st WMD We expected to leave but the order was countermanded. I was in a nettle all day to get out & did not. I bought & sold a pair of boots made 25. I sold a blanket for 25 & bought a watch for 2,50, a shirt for 12. I then packed my box to send to Father. We got our guns and were drilled with them as Co's and a Regt, we were presented with a flag. There was a light shower while the speech was being delivered. I was drilled till my arm ached xc.
T 2nd RD I wrote a let for Lewis Tarbel[48] and sent a box of things to Father but could not get out to see to it (send it). I was in a fret all day. Very heavy rain AM. At 3 PM we were called out for for a napsack drill and put through till 5. We were then m(arched) into the R and to the steam boat.[49] O how muddy it was much. Such a time as we had last fall at L(ittle) Falls at the Wide awake meeting As soon as we were on were under motion for NY on our way to Wsht. We were soon stoped in a sand bed and had to be toed off. I felt very hungrery. We got our sup and at 9 we took our bed on the deck. I rested well but was waked often. So the first N(ight).

[*Editor's Note*. It appears that William McLean was a member of the Wide Awakes as evidenced by his referencing them telling about the "time we had last fall...at the Wide Awake meeting." He certainly was in attendance in the fall of 1860 in Little Falls and was likely a member of the group.

48. Lewis Tarbel (19) enlisted May 1 at Norway, mustered into Co. C.
49. The regiment took the steamer Western World from a wharf in the lower part of the city.

"The Wide Awakes" were paramilitary campaign organizations affiliated with the Republican Party during the United States presidential election of 1860. The term "Wide Awakes" became popular in the 1860 campaign. The standard Wide Awake uniform consisted of a full robe or cape, a black glazed hat, and a torch six feet in length to which a large, flaming, pivoting whale-oil container was mounted. Its activities were conducted primarily in the evening and consisted of several night-time torch-lit marches through cities in the northeast and border states. The Wide Awakes adopted the image of a large eyeball as their standard banner.

Typical Wide Awakes chapters also adopted an unofficial mission statement. The following example comes from the Chicago Chapter:

1. To act as a political police.
2. To do escort duty to all prominent Republican speakers who visit our place to address our citizens.
3. To attend all public meetings in a body and see that order is kept and that the speaker and meeting is not disturbed.
4. To attend the polls and see that justice is done to every legal voter.
5. To conduct themselves in such a manner as to induce all Republicans to join them.
6. To be a body joined together in large numbers to work for the good of the Republican Ticket.

In 1860, the New York Herald estimated that there were over 400,000 drilled and uniformed Wide-awakes, nationwide.] (Source: Wikipedia)

W 3 WD When I awoke I found myself under motion and was highly entertained with the scenery of the highlands and Catskill Mountains, West Point and so on till we came to the swamp like harbor of NY. This is easer (easier) seen then described. At ½ past 1 we cast anchor and lay round till ½ p(ast) 8 on the 4th. There was a deal of excitement. I had 20'00 dollars changed for a gold piece. I did not rest well.

Th 4th WD At 8 ½ we left NY and went to Elizabethtown. Here we got some cold water and some of the boys got licquear and were tight enough. At 11 ½ we took our rout(e) through New Jersey, then through Penn(sylvania) and so on all night. We stoped after and I got off and felt at liberty.

F 5 WD I felt tip top though I did not sleep much. We kept on till 11 then we stoped and got some sasaphras and crossed the line into Maryland. I had not seen so good buildings or land as in Maryland since I left NY. Grain was ripe & cut all the way. When we got to Myld we expected to fight or at least to see the secesion flag. But we were haled with joy and the stars and stripes waved on every pole and house tops. Our expectations were all blasted when we got to Baltimore. Here we were to meet with opsition we thought but all was on our side. No flag but the stars and stripes. We were saluted with kindness and stayed from 2 ½ till 5 ½. Then we went on after m(arching) through the city to Washington in good cars. There were a long train. There were 7000 soldiers in B(altimore) city and encampments all the way to Wh (Washington). We got to Wh at 10 PM.[50] We were asleep a mile from the depot in a good room.[51] We rested well xc xc xc +

S 6th I went to the Capitol of the US and was much interested in viewing its halls xc. The paintings and engravings were splendid. I viewed the place till satisfied then I went into the front yeard or grove and wrote some in my diary. Then I lay down a while. I went to the quarters and eat 2 or 3 dry crackers, lay round a while then went to the Cap(ital) again. There had been a zouave shot last N at a whorehouse,[52] the murder(er) could not be found out. The boys, to have revenge, went to the house and burnt it to the ground. I went to it and was standing in the rode(road) with the crowd when 50 cavelry came through the crowd on a gallop. O! what a scattering, how we scaled a picket fence and went into an orchard. The cavelry kept all straight after they came. There was a large crowd on the fence and the horsemen come into the orchard and chased us out with their swords drawn and guns and revolvers all loaded at their side. They took some prisoners for not runing. O how feirce they looked. I drank 4 beers & felt grand.

50. In its July 6 edition, the Washington Intelligencer reported that "The Thirty-fourth Regiment, New York State Volunteers, arrived here at nine o'clock last evening. It is a fine body of men, who are mostly from Herkimer County. The regiment numbers a thousand men."
51. The 34th was initially put up in rooms in the vicinity of 9th & D Streets, NW.
52. This is likely the area now called the Federal Triangle; then populated with many such houses.

Washington City, circa 1860. Note the railroad station, three blocks north of the Capitol and the roads leading northwest from the city near the Potomac River (Source: Library of Congress).

Sab 7 WD We had a few crackers for brf. I got some soup -5 and at 8 A.M. we were in line to m(arch). We went S two miles and then laid down the things to encamp. We were a hot mess of boys. Some of them were sunstruck xc. I went to see Mr. Corneilous Westman who was in Col. McQuades Regt and found him sick. I came back and saw 20 baggage wagons drawn by 4 horses each and the drivers rode 2nd high horse and drove with one line. At 1 PM we took our napsacks and all of the baggage of a soldier which is about 50 lbs, being dissatisfied with our locality & m(arched) a mile farther & pitched our tents on a hill surrounded by woods.

we had for our supper one cracker and a piece of pork. I went in to swim. I drank a deal of water & We each had one cracker for tea and a piece of pork. At 12 M there was a shot fired at the guard. We were called up and soon found all was well, we then lay down again & was up again in an hour. We did nothing this time. Some well frightened.

[*Editor's Note*. Cornelius Westman was from Deerfield, NY and a student at Fairfield Seminary in 1861. Westman, 26 years old, enlisted May 1, 1861 at Booneville, NY as a private. He was mustered into Company F of the 14th New York Infantry on May 17. The 14th Infantry, known as the 1st Oneida County regiment was organized at Utica, NY. The 14th contained five companies from that city, one from Rome, one from Boonville, one from Syracuse, one from Lowville, and one from Hudson. Its colonel was James McQuade. The 14th NY left the state for Washington on June 18,1861. For a month the 14th regiment was stationed on Meridian Hill, now a park in upper northwest DC, along 16th Street. Cornelius Westman survived the war and was mustered out on May 24, 1863 at Utica, NY.
The camp of the 34th was named Camp Kalorama which was on the heights outside the city limits of Washington City and north of Meridian Hill. Today this area is known as Kalorama Heights and is located in upper northwest DC. The mansion was at approximately 23rd and S Street, NW. In 1807, the noted poet Joel Barlow bought a local property and mansion and renamed it "Kalorama," which translates from Greek as "fine view." Barlow lived in the home until shortly before his death in 1812. Barlow commissioned White House architect Benjamin Latrobe to enlarge the house and elevate its design.
A description of the property was written by Surgeon Alfred Castleman of the 5th Wisconsin when he passed through the area in late September 1861. His description reads, "it is one of the most magnificent places that imagination can picture. You enter the large gate, guarded by a beautiful white cottage for the janitor, and by a circuitous route through a dense grove of deciduous and evergreen forest, you rise, rise, rise, by easy and gradual ascent, the great swell of ground on which stands the beautiful mansion, shut out from the view of the visitor till he is almost on the threshold, but overlooking even its whole growth of forest, and the whole country for miles around." Kalorama (the residence) was destroyed by a fire during the Civil War while it was being used as a Union hospital.]

M 8th WD I had nothing to eat till 6 ½ P.M. I wrote a letter to father and Simpson. We had a dress parade AM. All goes well now.

In this circa 1865 photo, the burned Kalorama Mansion is on the left. (Source: Google Images).

T 9 WD I wrote to B. J. Hine. And went in to swim. There was a shower at 6. All goes well. We took a prisoner this morning.

W 10 I wrote to Uncle John, Miss M.J.G. & Miss R. Northrup. There was a shower at (undetermined number) all goes well.

Th 11 PD I went to W.D.C. city and made the white house a visit. I was in the hot house (greenhouse). There was a great many flowers. I saw his team[53] his sons and went into his reception room. It was a beautiful place but it was very plain. I went to the capitol. Congress was in session. I went into the cenete (Senate) chamber then coming down I got lost and after a long search found myself in the back yeard. I was 15 minutes getting into the front again. I got oysters xc = 05 I got paper = 26. Then went back to camp came in D.P.

F 12th Wrote a let to H.B. Ellis and was on guard 24 hours, 4 of them in the m from 9 till one, then from 4 till till 7AM in a heavy rain. I like to stand guard but not in the rain.

53. In 1861 the White House had a greenhouse and a stable beside it.

White House, south view with the "hot house" on left, ca. 1865. (Source: Author's collection).

S 13 I wrote a let for Bill Salisbury[54] and one for MB Hayes.[55] We drilled at 4 PM. I shot at a mark in AM. All goes well. We had a drill at 1 and Rev Van Petten[56] with us. He prayed at the close of the drill.

Sab 14th I wrote 2 let and went to hear a sermon at 6 PM. I heard that Mrs. Halle was dead. Our tent was Solm (solemn).

M 15 I went in to swim & wrote a let to Miss M.A. Davis. We were marched to the city of W to escort a Regt that left by the side of us. We were awful tired when we come back. I got a floor for our tent from one of the men that left, all of our boys got floors. We had a busy day.

T 16 WD We were called up last night at 1 oclock. There was an alarm given out at some other camp. We were soon releved and we

---

54. William A. Salisbury (19) enlisted May 1 at Norway, mustered into Co. C; later killed at Antietam.
55. Martin V. B. Hayes (22) enlisted May 5 at Graysville, mustered into Co. C.
56. Chaplain John B. Van Petten was the principal of the large and prosperous Fairfield Seminary. He resigned his position to become the first chaplain of the regiment. Van Petten had an influence on many of the young men from Fairfield joining the regiment.

then rested well. At our first morning drill the tents were inspected for to find stolen property, we were to get 4 weeks in the guard house with a ball on our leg, fed on bread and water for stealing any thing from each other. We were drilled very hard.

W17 WD I (wrote) a let to Mr Moody, one for J Hogan.[57] We had a hard drill at night which gave me the dire (diarrhea) very badly. I was up in the night.

Th 18 WD I went to the docter and got some powders. I did not have to drill. I lay round.

F 19 WD I was on the sick list. There was no drilling to day till dress parade on the account of a young man in Co. K getting shot by his own revolver which fell from his pocket and discharged. The ball entered his right brest. He died instantanously, he only said, "O God, I am shot." (his name was Waterhouse from Coopertown). I lay round all day.

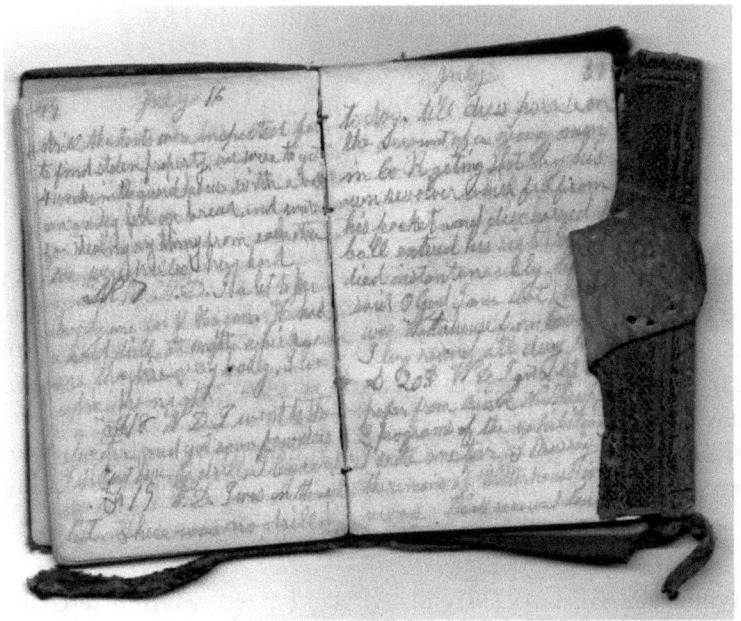

Diary pages for July 17 – July 20. (Source: Author's collection).

57. John Hogan (35) enlisted May 15 at Salisbury, mustered into Co. C; later discharged for disability.

July 1861   57

[*Editor's Note*. From the regimental history: "George J. Waterhouse, of Company K, going to the brook in the morning, to fill his canteen, leaned over, his revolver slipped from his side coat pocket, the hammer struck on a stone, the pistol was discharged, and the ball passed directly through his heart. Waterhouse was a printer, employed in the office of the Little Falls Journal (also identified as the Herkimer County Journal), at the time of his enlistment. His tragic death produced a profound impression." George Waterhouse was 20 years old and enlisted May 1 at Albany. Waterhouse was the 34th's correspondent to the newspaper. Lt. William Walton became the correspondent to the Journal after the death of Waterhouse.]

S 20th WD I got a let and paper from Miss R Northrup with 3 programs of the exhibition. I wrote one for T. Murrey[58] & the remains of Waterhouse was taken away. We all received linin pants. All went off well.

Sab 21 I wrote a let to R Bass (or Barr). I lay round some. PM we listined to a patriotic sermon, 1 oclock and received m(arching) orders before we got to our tents. There has been hard fighting within hearing of us to day.[59] The rour of the cannon has filed the Air with her horse (hoarse) echoes. The orders to march were countermanded. I wrote a let for L Tarble. All is excitement.

[*Editor's Note*. One of the other soldiers writing letters home was Private Solomon B. Clark of Company I. Clark was 26 years old and had enlisted May 22 at Hammondsport. He may not have known William McLean except in passing as their companies would have been camped some distance apart, though at the same site. His letter copied below was written prior to the "march" order being countermanded. It is clear from his letter that there was considerable speculation as to the future movements of the regiment. Clark would later die on June 1, 1862 of wounds received in the Battle of Fair Oaks on the previous day. His letter to his parents is published here for the first time. Note that at the time Clark wrote the letter, he was unaware of the horrendous defeat suffered by the Union forces.]

58. Thomas Murry (44) enlisted May 1 at Russia, mustered into Co C, discharged for disability July 28, 1861.
59. Battle of Bull Run fought Sunday July 21, 1861 resulting in a Confederate victory.

Washington D.C. (Sunday) July 21/61
Head Quartes 34 Reg N.Y.V.

Dear Parents
I have a few moments to write you. We are ordered to provide ourselves with two days rations and lay on our arms ready to march at a moments notice. They have had a big battle to-day at Bull Run near Manassas Junction have been successful, and we rec'd orders to march immediately. So we packed up shouldered knapsacks and started out when orders came again to provide as above. We march before morning & possibly not until then. If we go into Virginia we shall be in the enemies lines and perhaps I shall have no opportunity of writing then but will do so as soon as possibly and let you know of my whereabouts. We shall probably go to Manassas and from there to Richmond. There has got to be some hard fighting and pray the Lord to help the right. You can write and direct as before and I guess they will be forwarded.

Truly Your Affectionate Son
S.B. Clark
Co I,34 Reg't, N.Y.S.V.]

M 22 RD We got our Rifles[60] in exchange for the muskets we had. All was packed & we were ready to take our march at 9 oclock and expected to go but did not. I went on guard and was in the rain 9 hours out of the 12 I stood. This makes out 24 hours that I had been on guard and 12 of them in heavy rain. There was a great deal of excitement about the battle of Sab(bath). Our troops were coming into the city in great multitudes many of them bleeding and weak from hunger. They had retreated in every direction and they came back in squads and by the single one. Thousands of our men were killed.

T 23rd I felt quite ill all D(ay). Our Regt had no supper, there was nothing in the city to be had. There were so many retreated soldiers in the city and New comers. I bought something to eat. All is excitement yet. Soldiers are coming in every hour weak with hunger and fatigued with their long retreat through wood and field.

60. These were Enfield rifles exchanged for the Model 1842 Springfield smoothbore muskets initially issued. Colonel Suiter had applied to NY Governor Morgan for "more efficient arms". (Regimental history)

24th WD I feel better but went to the Dr and got some powder. Then I went out to write. We got no breakfast from the same reason. So goes a soldiers life. I got a let from B F Hine. All is well.

Th 25 I wrote a let to B F H(ine) and sent him two papers, & one to father and J Lawton. I got 3, one from Uncle John and Mother AM & one from Father PM. Father and Brother are not at home. I have felt quite well to D. The Dr. excused me from drill.

F 26 I wrote a let to Simpson. Then passed the guard and went to the city. I stroaled around all D & talked with those that had been in the battle of Sabbath. I returned at 3 oclock and passed the guard again. All went off well. WD

S 27 WD I wrote a let for M.B Hayes and drilled for the first time since last Thursday.

Sab 28 I was on guard but felt rather poorly. We had a heavy shower at 6PM just as we came off of guard. For we were on 3 hours and off 3. I felt well in the night.

M 29 I lay round till 3 oclock. Packed my things & then 35 baggage wagons come to move us. (very warm). We expected to be M off forthwith but we fooled round til M. There was a sight of burning brush & some singing, shouting and cooking xc xc. All was excitement, our tent went to sleep as cool as ever.

[*Editor's Note.* On Monday, July 29, 19-year-old Private Albert G. Easterbrook, Co. G, went into the city, probably with other members of his company, and had his image made at an undetermined picture gallery. Easterbrook is standing stoically at attention in the early uniform of the 34th. He is holding a long-tassled, beanie-like cap with his uniform pants tucked into his boots. He appears to have a paper of some sort (perhaps a letter) tucked into his shirt. This image was surely sent home.
Easterbrook enlisted the previous May 1 at Oneida, NY. He was killed in action at Antietam near the Dunker Church, September 17, 1862. His grave is not among those identified of the 34th at the National Cemetery at Sharpsburg.]

T 30 At daylight we were up and eat brft, halled down our tents and packed them in order. We were expecting to (move) every moment til 9 A.M. Then we started in the heat of the suthern sun and

Albert Easterbrook shortly after receiving his uniform.
(Source: American Civil War Database).

M through Georgetown an(d) southwest[61] for the space of 2 hours. Then we stopped at a small village viz Tennertown. It was located on a pleasant hill which afforded a shool (school) house, a meeting house, and grocery store with the aid of a saloon or 2.

[*Editor's Note*. In 1790, Washington locals began calling the neighborhood "Tennally's Town" after area tavern owner John Tennally. Over time, the spelling has evolved and by the 19th century the area was commonly written as Tenallytown, although the spelling Tennallytown continued to be used for some time in certain capacities, including streetcars through the 1920s. The current accepted spelling is Tenleytown. The area is the site of Fort Reno, one of the forts that formed a ring around Washington D.C. during the Civil War to protect the capital against invasions. It proved

61. Georgetown was west of the camp of the 34th NY. To reach Tennallytown from Georgetown, travel would be north-northeast.

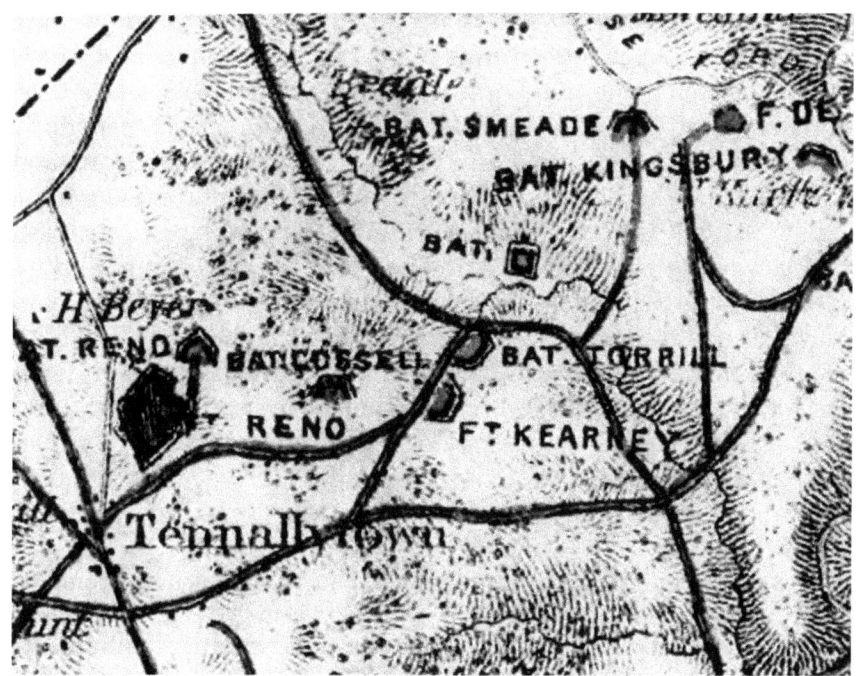

Map showing Tennallytown area. Fortifications shown built post-1861. (Source: Library of Congress).

to be the crucial lookout point for preventing a siege of Washington (indeed, it is the highest natural point in the District of Columbia). Fort Reno was decommissioned with the surrender of the Confederate armies. In the post-Civil War era, the Fort Reno area was a free black community. This community was almost entirely wiped out when the federal government decided to condemn most of its housing to build Deal Middle School, Wilson High School, a park, and a water tower. The Jesse Lee Reno school building, which housed an African-American school during the Jim Crow era, is one of the few remaining traces of this history. Within the park boundaries lies the highest natural point in the District of Columbia, 429 feet above sea level.] (Source: Wikipedia)

We halted here and eat our dinner ration which we had in our haversacks, in a very cool grove, or wood at the west of the village.

After resting an hour we took up our time of march again[62] and proceeded in open order (arms at will) for a distance of 4 miles. Again we rested and filled our canteens with cool water at a spring which seemed to have been placed there for our special benefit by the Creator. Thus for this PM. The road had been hilly strong and very rough. When we come to a stream if we could not leep it we had to wade it for there was no bridges. The fences were enclosed by blackbery bushes hanging down with ripe berries and our boys improved the privelage of satisfying their apetites. I felt leg weary and took the pleasure of going ahead with some of the other boys & eat all the berries I could & stopped once and got all the (undetermined) milk I could drink. I was ahead till we stoped at a beautiful cold spring in a pleasant wood. We were tired and slept poorly as we had no covering. I was cold. Our bagg(age) wagons were with us and one of the horses died xc.

[*Editor's Note*. Upon the first regimental organization which was completed at Albany, 40-year-old John B. Van Petten was mustered in as chaplain of the 34th. Shortly thereafter he began furnishing reports about the 34th to the Utica (NY) Morning Herald. The following is one of his first reports written on August 8 about the movement of the 34th on Tuesday, July 30.

SENECA MILLS, MD., HEADQUARTERS 34TH
REGT., N. Y. S. V., August 8, 1861.
To the Editor of the Utica Morning Herald:

As we anticipated when I wrote you last, we left Kalorama, Washington, DC, Tuesday, July 30, at 9 o'clock, A. M. There were no incidents of interest on the march, and having left three companies under Major Laflin at Big Falls, on the 31st, we reached Seneca Mills on the 1st of August, with seven companies, under Lieut.-Col. Suiter. We had quite a heavy baggage train, with many poor teamsters and a bad road, and hence we made rather a slow march. But as there was no visible foe in our neighborhood, it was all right. Our guide was Mr. C. G. Sage, formerly of Central New York, who is a resident of Virginia, and a thorough Union man.

62. They would have been marching along present day River Road in Montgomery County, MD. Lt. William Walton in his report to the Journal, says "leaving the city we took the Potomac river road."

He was the guide of McDowell at Bull's Run, and was in the thickest of that ill starred battle. He rides a very fine, strong and fleet cream stallion, which goes like a deer through the woods, leaps fences and swims canals and rivers. Mr. Sage, upon his noble steed, was pursued for three miles by five cavaliers, who emerged suddenly from the woods between Bull's Run and Fairfax. But the pursuit was vain. Had it been successful it might have cost the pursuers dear, as Mr. Sage is an unerring shot and a man of great coolness and courage. He is to remain with us to act as guide and messenger.]

W 31 WD A last D(ay). We eat our brft and started at 7 oclock AM. We were kept in ranks and M slowly, stoped often and at ten AM we were once more in an open field close to the edge of a lite pine wood and soon began to cook our noonday meal here. We refreshed ourselves and 3 cos of our Regt were taken from us and stationed 3 miles distance at the Potomac to guard the water works & canal, at the great falls.[63] We are now in Montgomery Co. M(arched) paralal with the River 5 miles to the north through as poor a section of Country as ever I traveled. The fields were very few and poor. The houses mostly small framed buildings, white washed on the outside, some log huts & some stone which looked as if they had been built about the year one. The principle body of the land was covered with small pines all of 2nd growth which covered the land that had been worn out years ago by the poisineous weed tobaco & slave labor. While the Reg't tarried, I scouted around went to a school house which was very nete (neat) and clean, though of logs. It was built and perhaps (by) the great grandfathers of the ch(urch) which now attend once attend the some in the same style. On my tramp I went to a secession house with some other boys and had some bread and butter to eat. At 5 PM we were once more under

63. Companies B, G, and I under the command of Major Byron Laflin were detached to guard the Chesapeake & Ohio (C&O) Canal and the Water Works at Great Falls, MD. The Water Works was the water supply for the city of Washington.

march. I went with a scermishing party which went in advance of the Regt to see if all is right. After a M of 3 miles the shade of M were upon us and we took lodgings on a very nice side hill in a grove with a good supply of cold water. We soon had eaten our supper then we sprauled out on the y[ard] with a rubber blanket for beding. Soon we were asleep. But ere long there was a heavy shower and we were roused. Some were wet and some kept of[f] the rain by sitting up & covering with their blankets.

Entrance to Water Works at Great Falls, circa 1861-1865 (Library of Congress)

CHAPTER VII

August 1861; Camp Jackson, Darnestown, and Preparing for Action

August 1861

August 1st Th At day break we started on to our destination not stoping to cook any but we only eat some crackers. Ere we had proceeded far on our hilly journey with the trees nearly meeting each other across the road though they were very small pines. Another very heavy southern shower wet us in a complete soke. I and many others left the ranks and went on ahead pick blackberries and huckle b(erries). I had all I wished to eat sometimes I was alone out of sight and hearing of our men. I know I was in an enemies land but still entured on without fear. At 10 AM we were safe at our camping ground though very well tired, not withstanding we had M but 20 mi(les). Our tents were soon picked and dinner cooked. I was chosen for guard but did not have to stand til 10 PM. The PM was spent in cleaning our guns and shoting. I took the meat out of a turtle shell xc xc.

F 2nd WD I am sitting on my post in an open field and am writing my di(a)ry. The sun is just up and I have written 5 pages. Soon I was released and had the pleasure of seeing 4 men that we had taken prisoners, also a gun and sword. Two of them were releeced after brf and two were kept. I went with H. Greenly a mite from the camp and got some blackberries, shot a chipmunk xc. I lay in the woods and tried to sleep in the heat but I could not take any comfort. We had dress parade at 7 PM and then learned that our camp was named Jackson,[64] Senecka (Seneca) Mills, Darnestown,

64. Though the exact location of Camp Jackson is not specified, it was likely in the vicinity of what is now River Road and Seneca Road near Riley's Lock Road.

Montgomery Co. Soon the shades of N(ight) were blinding us, and the music of tree toads were charming us and sing some to sleep. While two of my friends & myself were trying to pass the gu[ard], one of them said he had the countersighn[65] but to our disapointment and fright our friend had not the right word X. We were kept at the point of the benet (bayonet) till the sergent of the guard was called for. He did not come and we we(re) let go back after a short time. We then heard the report of guns by our guard in every direction.

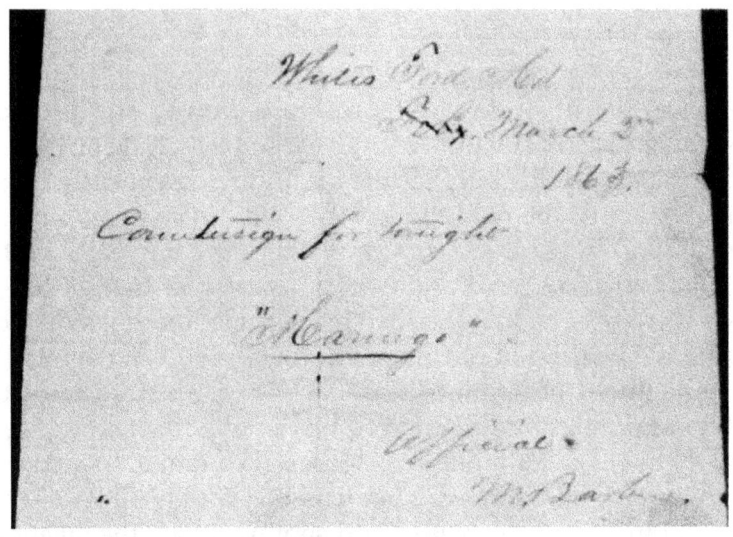

Written Countersign for March 3, 1864 at White's Ford, MD near Seneca Mills. White's Ford was a Potomac River crossing point for troops of both armies. (Source: Author's collection).

S 3rd WD This morning I volunteered to go and guard the cannal with 2 of our Co boys. There were 5 going out of each Co stationed for a space of 4 miles along the river to keep the Rebbles from crossing (and) to stop the boats on the canal which was about

65. In order to pass through the picket line, a soldier had to know the "countersign" word in answer to the "parole" word offered by the sentry. Not knowing the countersign would not allow you to pass and could subject you to arrest within the regiment. Daily orders specified the parole and countersign in writing to officers.

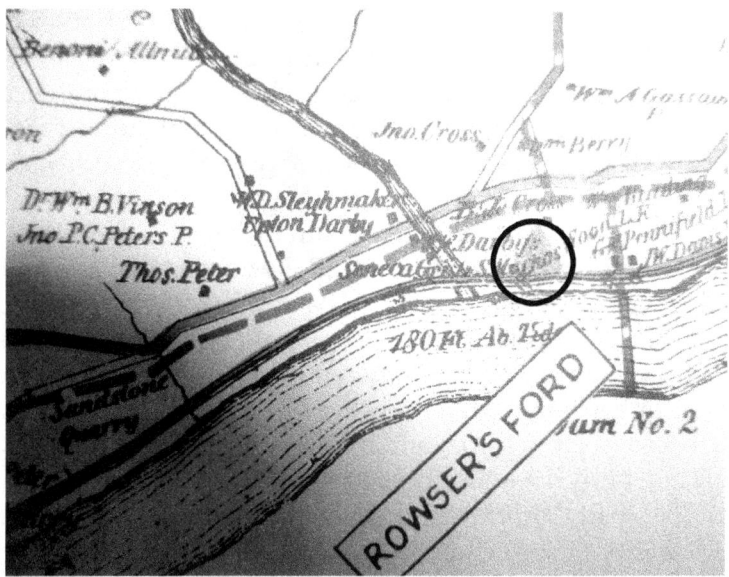

The triangle above Rowser's Ford shows the location of the Seneca Mills Camp. (Source: The Library of Congress).

ten rods north of the river. We were stationed[66] at our posts at one PM & I started for water with 3 canteens. I had to cross the Canal to get it so I undertook to swim it with my pants and shirt on my head. When I launched off, I found my clothes on my back sailing in the water. Also my wach was in my pocket. Well I rung my clothes and put them on. Just (as) I got them back they took another soaking. I then got some boards and plank and rails and grape vines and made a raft. We picked a host of berries and felt quite out of prison, but had to wach the river to keep sciffs from crossing, but saw none. All well.

 Sab 4[67] WD I got 2 lets, one L A Brocket[68] & Miss M A Davis. I read them ling [lying] on my blanket between the river & C(anal).

66. From the regimental history, "the regiment now has the custody of about seventeen miles of river-front...from a point two miles east of Great Falls to eight miles west of Seneca Mills".
67. On August 4th, the 34th was attached to Stone's Brigade, Division of the Potomac for outpost duty on the Upper Potomac.
68. This is probably Leonard A. Brockett (33) of Salisbury.

This did not seem much like the sab. I went (with) another fellow and got a haversack full of aples and potatos from an old Rebble and also a turkey that would weigh 15 lbs. I shot at him twice and pecked him. This Reble owned 90 slaves of male kind that were able working men, beside all the rest of his young and females. So goes the Sabbath.

 M 5 W AM We found our sabbath turkey all covered with flie blowes & bugs. We threw it into the R. I went to camp and crackers xc. There was a heavy shower at 6 PM. We fished some.

 T 6th I had the pleasure of sleeping on a little stoney cape last N to escape the wet. The stones were the sise of potatoes, and the bed was rather hard. I felt bad this M. At 12 last night, 4 of our men crossed the R in a boat and set fire to a small house and wheet stack. They burn the house because it was a shelter to Reble picket guard.[69] I lay in the sun with a severe headache and went to camp at 4 PM and sent back a man in my place. When I left the picket our boys were shooting accross the R at a house thinking that there had been a shot from it. I have a high fevor and headache.

[*Editor's Note*. This same incident is recorded in Distant Drums, Chapter 1, page 11:

> On the Virginia side of the Potomac, opposite the 34th were three or four houses that sheltered rebels taking "pot-shots" at the Union pickets. To remedy the situation, James Faville of Salisbury and Johnny Johnson from Little Falls, nicknamed the "infants" because they stood well over six feet tall and the McLaughlin brothers, Robert and John from Salisbury, boated across the river one night and set fire to the houses. the enemy sharpshooters fled and the quartet from the 34th started back across the river barely escaping a band of angry rebels. No shots were fired until trigger happy Federal pickets fired at the Herkimer County boys. Fortunately their aim wasn't very good and the men made it back safely.

In addition, Chaplain John B. Van Petten also reported this incident to the Utica Morning Herald in his letter of August 8. His account reads, "In this

---

69. This incident is not recorded in the regimental history. It is the first mention of any of the men of the 34th crossing the river.

letter I will inform you of rather a thrilling incident which occurred night before last. Just opposite Seneca Mills Lock, across the Potomac, stood an old house and a few other buildings which had been occupied by rebels as a covert from which to fire on our pickets, and annoy the lock tender and family. It occurred to several of us that the nuisance should be removed. Hence James Fanell (sic Faville), John Johnson, Robert McLaughlin and John McLaughlin, of Company K, (Capt. Beverly) volunteered to do the work. About 8 o'clock P. M. they launched an old skiff and started for the old Virginia shore. They stole quietly along when they had reached the shore, until they had reached the desired point, when soon the flames of the old rebels' nest illumined the water and the sky. Just then a heavy signal gun was fired on the enemy's side, to give notice, doubtless, to his troops in the vicinity. But the brave boys did up their work well, and pulled for the Maryland side, which they reached with safety."]

W 7 I wrote a let to Uncle John and felt the same. All went of hard.

Th 8 Headache still. I got more powders from the Dr.[70] Another Regt came and camped by the side of us.[71]

[*Editor's Note*. In his August 8 letter to the Utica Morning Herald, John B. Van Petten commented on the regiment that camped beside the 34th. He writes:

Governor Gorman, of Minnesota, arrived with his Regiment at this place yesterday. As the senior Colonel he is to command, as we understand, the troops between Washington and Harper's Ferry. He is to act, we believe, as Brigadier General in this region. He is an active, energetic man, who has seen considerable service. He was in the Mexican war, and participated in the principal battles. He entered that war as Captain, and by his courage and other high qualities, attained the rank of Colonel. He was in the terrible fight at Bull's Run, and occupied the extreme right of Col. Heintzelman's division. His regiment was the nucleus about which the Fire Zouaves rallied after they had been broken and lost most of their officers, and had much to do with the annihilation of the

70. This would either be the regimental Surgeon, Socrates N. Sherman or the Assistant Surgeon Edward S. Walker.
71. Various records indicate there were as many as 18,000 Federal soldiers at Camp Jackson.

black horse cavalry. This regiment, also, though it lost in killed and wounded as many as any other in the field, came off in good order, and was very soon ready for efficient service. Though there is naturally just now, great distrust of our leaders, yet we are confident that the Governor will be a good Brigadier.

Private Solomon B. Clark, Company I, was with one of the three companies detailed to guard the Water Works at Great Falls. They were under the command of Major Byron Laflin. Their camp was aptly named Camp Washington. He is writing home to his family from their camp.

Camp Washington, Great Falls Md
Aug 8 1861

Dear Friends at Home
I received (undetermined) letters with many thanks. You would think the soldier longed for letters from home, could you see them when the mail comes in. There is no mail carriers here, only as it is carried by private conveyance. One of the officers generally goes down to Washington for it two or three times a week. But Fred St. John[72] is going home on a furlough tomorrow and I though to send this by him. He is miserable and think it will do him good to go home for 20 days.
We have not heard from Cap't King[73] yet only that he advertized to leave H'port last Thursday. You have probably sent a letter by him. At least hope so, and if you can see Fred you can send by him also, but please do not wait for him before you send any.
We are having very good times here. The boys are generally feel better and are healthier than I think they were at Kalorama Heights. The only real complaint they make is the food. We do not get any bread here but hard crackers, so hard they have to be soaked before we eat them. But as we have tea or coffee most every meal I can get along first rate. I do not mind it at all.

72. Frederick B. St. John (25) enlisted May 22 at Hammondsport, NY. He was mustered into Co I June 15 for two years. The regimental history shows him as deserting August 1 at Great Falls. This date is obviously incorrect.
73. William H. King (26) enlisted May 22 at Hammondsport and was mustered into Co I as Captain on June 15. He was twice wounded May 31, 1862 at Fair Oaks, VA and resigned January 1, 1863 at Falmouth, VA.

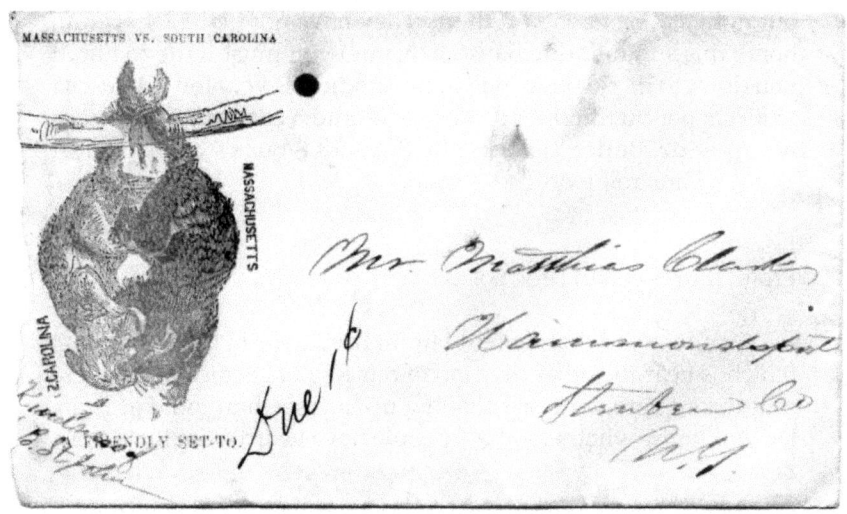

Envelope addressed by Solomon Clark to his father.
(Source: Author's collection).

Night before last we were routed out as one of the guards got shot through the leg by a pistol. He was close by the canal and thought it came from the other side. He returned the fire and then called for the officer of the guard. It occured about 10 oclock and we watched all night but saw nothing nor had any more disturbance. Yesterday it was murmured around that he shot himself so as to get a discharge. His pants and leg was burnt by the powder which would not have been had the shot been fired from the opposite side of the canal. But it is not known to be so, and it would be too bad to say so if that was not the case.

He is doing very well I believe as it was merely a flesh wound. Otherwise we have had no disturbance only some slave owners came and claimed some negroes we had here. One we had for cook and our picket brought in three others. They were given up by the Major.

Penn Ross[74] just brought in a letter for me from Sue. I will read it and let you know the news. They are not all well. Dan has been sick about three weeks but works some. Juddy is rather unwell

---

74. Penn Ross (21) enlisted May 22 at Reading Centre. He was mustered into Co I June 15 for 2 years. He was discharged for disability January 1, 1862 at Poolesville, MD.

but not very sick I should think. They have not had a letter from home this summer due days(?). (Name) you must write to him if you don't to me so often, will you? Produce is very low. Wheat 45 to 55 cts per bu. Butter 4 to 6 cts, eggs 4 to 5 cts per dz. Hen eggs are 2/per dz. Butter 31 cts per lb. Potatoes 8/bu. xc xc. But I must close as I am going on guard soon.

Love to all,
From Your Son and Bro. Sol

P.S. I understood that tonight Hiram Brink was in the Minn. Regt which is near the other division of our Reg't at Senica Mills, eight miles from here. I guess I shall go up and see him today if I can. Do you know whether _____ people have heard from him lately.
S.

The above letter was addressed by Solomon to his father, Mr. Mattias Clark, Hammondsport, Steuben Co., NY, and carried for delivery by Fred St. John. The corner of the envelope says "Kindness of Fred St. John", but also shows 1 cent postage being due. In 1860, Matthias Clark (57), a farmer, lived with his 52-year-old wife Sarah, his daughter Sarah (18), who was a school teacher and 26-year-old Solomon, also a farmer. The family had a live-in domestic, Angeline Van Ess, who was 40 years old.]

Fr 9 I was passed out. Got some berries, aples, peaches, corn, cucumbers, xc xc. I feel as usual.

S 10 I am on the sick list yet. I wrote a letter for A Warner.

Sab 11th I got 2 lets from Simpson & Father. I was on guard though I am no better.

M 12 MD I wrote to Simpson PM. I went out with some other boys and help ourselves to peaches, aples, tomatoes, corn, watermellon, and milk which belong to a friendly Reble.

T 13 Heavy rain, nothing particular hapens.

W 14 MD I got a pass from the col and went out with some of the boy. We went to a melon garden and helped ourselves to them. The proprietor come out and looked at us while we eat them. He did not like the sport. We then went a mile to the South and met a very smart darky. We talked with him a while and then went to the house. We were invited to eat which we did with pleasure. After a long conversation, we inquired how much our bill was, we were informed that it was nothing. But we had transgressed their rules & customs by talking with their servents. This is the way that slavery uses mankind an regulates customs. We returned to camp and filled our haversacks with peaches and corn. We had a long M at dress parade all round the fields and roads.

Th 15 I am on guard. We are all talking about the cold. There was a white frost last night and we hover close to the fire this morning. I went out again and got a man to stand 2 hours in my place (as we are 2 hours on and 4 off). We went to a negro shanty and bought some cakes and got milk. After we eat all we could, we got some aples then went into a barn and slept 2 or 3 hours. We then started for camp and filled our haver-sacks with corn on the way. When we got back we found our other 3 Co's of this Regt returned from the great Fall where they had been guarding.[75] I went on guard at 6 PM and had a chat with Myrt Zimmerman.[76] I was cold in the night. We have chily N(ight)s. All goes well now.

F 16 I wrote a let to father and examined a head. The Regt above us left. We cheered them heartly and they returned the compliment.

S 17 DD Some rain. I received a let from B F Hine and wrote one for L Tarbel, then lay around.

Sab 18 DD I chanced a pass and went out on it with another fellow, we roved round til noon then come to a house and asked for milk. We set down and talked a while and found the folks very sociable, and soon was invited to the table which was spred with hot cakes, milk, butter, xc. We were soon satisfied but had no bill to pay. We then come to another house got green corn by asking for it. We then returned to camp. I wrote a let to B F Hine. We had a sermon from Rev. J B Van Patten at dark from the text. "Remember now thy creator in the days of thy youth." We listened with attention Then we had dress pr by lantern light.

[*Editor's Note*. The bible verse, "Remember thy Creator in the days of thy youth" is taken from Ecclesiastes 12:1. This was a popular verse during

---

75. This was the return of Companies B, G, and I who were detached on July 31 to guard the water works at Great Falls.
76. Martin Zimmerman (18) of Little Falls, enlisted May 1 and was appointed as a Musician in the regiment.

the era which reminded the youth to pay attention to Godly things when young and avoid the excesses of youth. It was appropriate for the regimental chaplain to preach to the youth of the regiment on this topic. Curiously, this same verse is written and signed by Harriet Fenton behind the tintype of a young soldier who is likely Ezra D. Fenton. Ezra was 18 years old and enlisted in Company E on June 20, 1861 at Addison, NY. In 1861, Harriet Fenton (24) was married to Ezra's brother Jesse who was farming near Tuscarora in Steuben County, NY. Ezra later deserted at Seneca Mills, MD, on September 20, 1861. He never returned to his regiment, probably returned home, and continued to farm. Ezra was on his own as his father

Ezra Fenton in 1861

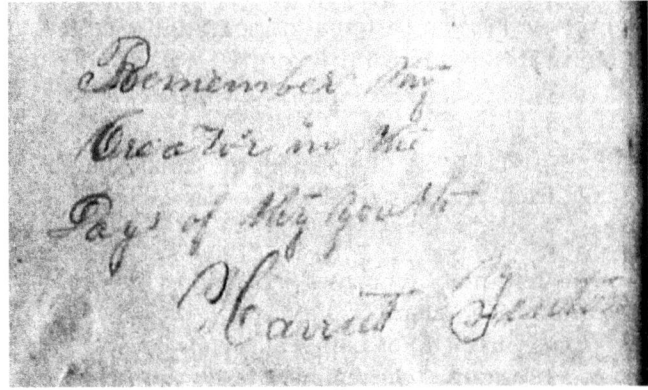

Harriet Fenton's quotation written in the case behind the image of Ezra Fenton. (Source: Author's collection).

had passed away in 1855. Ezra later married, fathered one son, and lived in the area until his death in 1914. He lies buried in the Orr Hill Cemetery in Tuscarora, NY.]

M 19th MD I was called on guard wrote a let to A. Young We had rain at 4 PM, just the time I went on guard. I caught some more cold & felt very badly. I went on guard again at 10 o'clock and could not stand up. I was so disy (dizzy) headed and sick to my stomach. I felt better afterward.

[*Editor's Note.* On Monday, August 19 Solomon Clark again writes home. Company I has now returned from its detail at the Water Works to join the rest of the regiment. Solomon expresses concerns and comments which most soldiers had when writing home; e.g. concern for family, friends and situation back home. He also takes time to tell of changes in command and suggest that some coffee sent to him may have been appropriated by some of the regimental officers. Lastly, he talks about friends from home forming additional companies. Enthusiasm for war service was still high.

Camp Jackson, Senica Mills, MD
August 19, 1861
Dear Friends at Home
Last Thursday we moved from Great Falls & joined the other part of the regiment at Senica Mills. We are very nicely situated here in the woods about ¾ of mile from the canal and river. It is about 21 miles from Washington. The Minnesota Reg't moved from here the day after we came. They have gone 9 miles up the river to Edwards Ferry. I saw Hiram Brink. He looks very thin having lost 30 lbs. He says he is going home when their three months is out which will be soon.[77] I should like to go also on a visit.

Your letter mailed on the 12th was received on the 15th with very many thanks. I had not heard from Mary(?) since I left Albany. And the sort letter tha Papa wrote did me a great deal of good. It was certainly more than I expected. Mother wrote a line

77. Hiram A. Brink (31) enlisted as a Private in Co. K of the 1st Minnesota Infantry on April 29, 1861. This was not a 90 day regiment. Hiram Brink was born in NY and his family lived near Bath in Steuben County where he met Solomon Clark. Hiram re-enlisted March 1, 1864 and transferred to the MN First Battalion Infantry.

in a previous letter for which I am very thankful. I wish she would write more.

It seems you have been making quite a deal in the horse and cattle line. I hope you have done well with Billy. You must have quite a good stock of cattle. It seems to me they will be good property before long. I do not know how much beef is now. There is a great deal of it used however. Who did you let have the bay colt? Any one in our neighborhood? If Mary will come home this fall I will try and meet her there if it is so I can.

I have not heard from Charley Mettza(?) since I came to Washington. I saw his Reg't pass once and they were in the battle,[78] but I do not know any thing about him. Nor Hiram Nyce(?). I should like to see him.

Our Reg't is under Brig. Gen. Stone now. We are under Gorman of Minnesota, Col. of that Reg't but he is under arrest now in Washington. Stone is under Major Gen. N.P. Banks who has command of Harpers Ferry & the upper Potomac. Cap't King returned the day before Fred St. John started home. He brought a large trunk full of cakes & cheese. I tell you, didn't we live. But that coffee you spoke of, I never saw it. Lena said part of it was for him also. A few days after we ate with the officers and we remembered the coffee. Why said we "when did you get this." That was before we knew there was any sent to him. He said it was the best coffee he ever drank. After I got your letter I spoke to Lt. Atwood[79] about having some coffee sent me but I did not get it. He asked if it was ground. I told him I did not know. That is all that was said about it. I think it was rather a mean caper. As to that Webber affair it is all gone now. The paper was sent here also one of the Penn Yan papers copied from the Courier. The boys tease him some. He has nothing to say in answer, only he tries to lay it on someone else. The whole Reg't knows it I guess. I had a letter _____ _____ not long ago. He said Cyrus had been getting up a company. Clark Bell must be sour I think. But it is about his style and if I knew he would open this I would write something for his own gratification. It has been raining here since four days. It is

---

78. This would be the first Battle of Bull Run when the 34th was camped in Washington.
79. Alfred T. Atwood (26) enrolled May 22 at Hammondsport. He was mustered into Co. I as 1st Lieutenant June 15. He mustered out with the regiment in Albany June 30, 1863.

none too warm here now. We have had some very warm weather, but I have seen it as warm in NY I think. I persieve we shall go to Harpers Ferry soon.
From your Son & Brother Sol]

T 20 PD The first we have had in an age. Our paymaster come and payed us 5.86. I colected a dollar.[80] The day was well occupied.[81]

[*Editor's Note*. The following two letters were written on August 20 from the camp of the 34th New York. They were written on the same sheet of stationery by two first cousins serving in Company F, Philip J. Crewell and John H. Crewell. Philip writes to a brother (unidentified) at home and John writes to his father. The 1855 New York State census shows P. Crewell (14) living with a 66-year-old J. Crewell (male) and 57-year-old A. Crewell (female). The penmanship on this record is clear and distinct. The 1860 Federal census does not show a Philip in the same household as his brother John. However the two Crewell households were adjacent to one another as recorded by the census takers in both 1855 and 1860. Philip was either not present or not recorded at the time of the 1860 census or perhaps away at school. However, Philip was not registered in Fairfield Academy for 1861.

John H. Crewell, 21, enlisted May 1 at Dennisons Corner and was mustered into Company F along with his cousin Philip, 20. Both John and Philip enlisted on the same day. The regimental history lists John as enlisting at Dennisons Corner and Philip enlisting at Columbia. Records indicate that these two locations were a short distance away in different hamlets in the same general area just south of Utica. John did not survive the war and died of disease on August 22 (regimental history) or 27 (New York State records), 1862 at Philadelphia, PA. New York State records show him as buried on August 31 at the Glenwood Cemetery, west of downtown Philadelphia. Philip was more fortunate and he mustered out with the regiment on June 30, 1863 at Albany at their expiration of service. Philip survived until 1917 and is buried in the Dennisons Corners Cemetery.

80. Probably refers to collecting money from those who owed him, as for examining heads for lice.
81. This was a bad day for the regiment. On this day James Cummins (19) Company I, died of disease and George Conch (19), also of Company I, deserted the regiment.

Philip begins the joint letter by writing to his unnamed brother. The page was then given to John who wrote to his father. As the farms were adjacent to one another, the letter was exchanged between the two families. Some of the information is the same in both letters. Minor corrections have been made to both letters for readability.

> Camp Jackson
> Senica Mills
> Montgomery Co, Maryland
> August 20th 1861
>
> Dear Brother
> I now sit down to write a few lines to you. I am well at present and hope these few lines may find you all the same. We have had not quite as good times as we had to the camp at Washington. We haven't had as good to eat but we have draud some money to day and I think that we will live a little better for a while. We draud $5 an 86 cents and the first of next month we draw $26 and I think that we will send some of that home, about $40 of it, that if we are any where we can get a check for it. I want you to write and let me know about the 14 Regiment whether there are any come home that you know of. They have had a site(?) at Washington about their two years. They wanted to get away in three months and they could not so we are told.[82] But we ain't no way we can hear the truth of the thing. I guess that there are some cowards among them. We are to have a battle in a few days by what I hear and the sooner the better it will be. So it will get settled some time or another. That all I can write now and I don't think that you can read this but you must try to make it out. We are all well and I hope we remain so.
> From your Brother
> Write as soon as you can.
> Philip Crewell

---

82. Apparently there was a dispute in the 14th NY about the length of their enlistment. The dispute took place while they were still in Washington City, before they moved up the canal.

The second letter on the same sheet is written by John H. Crewell.

> Camp Jackson
> Montgomery County MD
> August 20, 1861
>
> Dear Friend Father,
> I now take the pleasure of writing a few lines to you to let you know that I am well at present and I hope that when these few lines reaches you they will find you the same. We have get our pay today and get only $5.86 for 16 days now and the first of next month we get pay again then we get 26 dollars and Philip and I will send forty dollars home.[83] We have to stay two years if not sooner discharged. The boys said last week that they was a going to stack their arms the fifteen of next month but I guess they won't do it.[84] There has been a great deal of rain here. They think we will have an attack here in a few days. I have not received any letter since the one that DHC[85] wrote to me last week. I want you to let me know if 14 Regiment McQuade[86] has come home or not for they had a dispute about it here and if they have come home we will the fifteen of next month and if they hain't we won't till we get discharge. We have but poor living here now but we have got our pay so we can live better now. I won't send any money home for now I hain't got much. Give my love to all. No more at present.
> Good By
> From your son
> Direct as before, John H. Crewell]

83. This seems to indicate John and Philip were living in the same household. The 1860 Federal census does not record a Philip in the household. Philip could have been a middle name.
84. Apparently some of the men thought they had enlisted for 90 days.
85. DHC is the younger brother of John and Philip. His name was David. He was 18 in 1861.
86. There were three McQuades from Utica, NY in the 14 Regiment at this time. There ages were 31, 27, and 24. Two of the brothers were officers.

W 21 WD Our Regt moved 30 rods to a more healthy and pleasant place when I saw army things in my tent. I passed the guard and went to Darnestown. I spent a dollar very soon and returned to camp. I had a high fevor going and coming and I was very tired my joints ached awfuly. I have the fevargue. I got a check from W L Oswald[87] of 25 Dollars to send to L A Brockett. I suffered with pain.

Th 22 WD I went to the Dr. Though I felt better I only went for an excuse I wanted none of his medicine, but he gave me enough for two days. I did not take it, but I made some (medicine) to suit myself of veniger, cian pepper, sassafras bark and licqueor, it was good. I wrote a let to Leonard A. Brockett and sent a check of 25.00 dollars in it. I have a very hard cough and rais(e) flem from a very low part of my lungs, some fevor with a severe headache.

F 23rd WD Very cold morning. I cough more than usual. PM I have a chill I never ached so badly in my life.

S 24 PD I wrote a let to M A Davis and had another chills PM. O how bad

Sab 25 WD I feel hard. Us eat only fry(?) for breakfast, nothing alse all day. Had a very hard chill PM. The was a sermon preached but I could not attend.

M 26th All right AM, a chill PM. All dull.

T 27 This day has dawned and I have a craving appitite but nothing to eat but dry flour which we have the privelg of weting with cold water and frying in lard.[88] This goes rather tough though it is all we have had for bread these last 7 days. I tried to keep up but was obliged to wilt under another chill at 5 PM. I lay awake nearly all night.

W 28 MD I washed my person this M and felt worse, kept around but was not able to eat any breakfast though I buy milk biscakes & such things as I think I can relish. I sold my revolver for $8.50 to Rob Laughlin of Co. K.[89] I had a very light chill.

---

87. Captain W. L. Oswald, Company A, 29 years old, enrolled May 18 at West Troy. McLean does not explain why he is getting such a large check. May be pay being sent home.
88. This was how he made hardtack.
89. Robert McLaughlin (23) enlisted May 1 at Salisbury. Killed May 31, 1862 at Fair Oaks, VA.

Th 29 RD I lay around & bough[t] pie & milk, felt some better. We got our flour baked into good bread in our oven that Capt Soponabald[90] had built.

F 30 PD I went to the grist mill and weighed myself. I weighed 127. I then came to camp and wrote a letter to R. Northrup and lay round. I am feeling much better.

S 31 PD We had a general inspection of all our goods. Our things were all caried out of doors and our guns were inspected while we stood in line. I received 3 lets, one from father, brother, & B.F. Hine, I answere(d) fathers let and mailed it. I bought butter, serup and two diaries from the old sutter for 50 cts. I feel well to day, milk has recovered me. This month is used up and I have been sick the most of the time with a cold headache xc.

[*Editor's Note.* Private Philip Crewell, Company F, wrote a letter home to his brother on August 31 from Camp Jackson telling of some minor skirmishing that was going on in their area along the Potomac River. He also refers to some drinking and homesickness issues within the regiment. The length of service for the regiment is still on his mind, but he wants to do his duty and not be thought of as a coward or a disgrace to his family.

Camp Jackson Senica Mills
Montgomery Co Maryland
August the 31 1861

Dear Brother
I received a letter today and was glad to hear from home and all of you. I am well at present and have been since I left the other camp. John is well and all the rest of the boys. We are a having good times. The times all go off lively here now. We are in a good place where we can look over a great part of old Virginia and they do get watch as close as a cat would a mouse. We just came off guard yesterday, we have to guard the river for five miles and when we are down there we see a good many of the Rebels as some of them look for the last time when they come to them shores for our guns never lie to us now. I wrote John P. Banger[91] about their being

90. Captain Wells Sponable (31) enrolled May 1 at Little Falls, mustered in as Captain, Company B.
91. This individual cannot be identified. Spelling may be incorrect.

canons fired that morning that I wrote to him. It didn't amount to anything, they had a little brush just below us. They killed three on the other side and not one on our side. They tried to fool our men but they couldn't come it. They sent a niger on the other shore to draw our folks down to the shore so they would have a fair chance at them. Our folks went down and they had no more than got there then there was three of the rebels fired on them but their balls did not come acrost and that was the last time they ever pulled a trigger to a gun. The next moment they were kicking their last and the nigger was a white man in false dress. So you see how it came out, we are as safe as if we were in a fort. Now you heard that our company had been taken by eleven men. It is all false as there ain't eleven men of the South that can take us nor twice that amount. Don't believe half of what you hear for there is a good many lies told now in wartime. Now about our stacking arms. I don't think we will do it only for this one thing, that is for to get better officers but I am glad that it is as it is for they all had their one way and let them go. They are most all of them under an arrest for getting drunk. The Colonel and all our captains ain't been drunk. He ain't drinked any since he has bin a Captain and that one you said will hurt his whole regiment as you say for he can not go where there is any danger without me and the boys have repented the day they elected them. Lieutenant Shumaker[92] don't see a sober day when he can get the liquor. And now about Bill Manning.[93] They have taken no notes of it but whether he means to stay or not I don't know which he will do. Now he has been homesick enough to go home, well we would all like to see home, but we haven't his very long gone yet and I don't think that we will have to stay two years anyway. And as for fighting there won't be a fair fight nor any as the _____ is a wishing now for the

92. Joseph R. Shoemaker (28) enlisted at Herkimer on May 1. Mustered in as 1st Lieutenant in Company F. Shoemaker resigned July 26, 1862. Reason for his resignation is undetermined.
93. William Manning (24) enlisted May 10 at Herkimer. He was mustered in as a Corporal in Company G, later promoted to sergeant. Whatever thoughts of desertion he may have had did not result in taking action. He was mustered out with the regiment at the expiration of two years service.

South has offered 3 millions of dollars to settle the thing that is a letter he sent to _____. Whether it is so or not I can't tell. Their are over seven hundred thousand troops that has reported at head quarters now. There are 18 thousand here where we be that is within five miles and that is close enough for so many of us until we have to fight and that won't be here. I thought one spell that it would be but it seems to die away and I hope it may but if there is a battle here you won't see old Columbia disgraced nor the name of our family. Now tell mother not to feel so bad as I know the _____ for I think of you all a thousand times a day and that I long to see you all but I would not leave and have it said that I was a coward for a good deal. Thats all except that about that name you said you couldn't make out. You must put on specks and then you can read it. It is all right I guess you could read it. I will write some more _____ to you soon again. Some I want you to have. I haven't time nor paper as you can see.
Your Brother
Philip Crewell]

CHAPTER VIII

September and Early October 1861; First Action, Incursion Into Virginia

September, 1861

Sab 1st There was a young man in Co. H[94] shot this m before sunrise by his friend which was playing with him. I suppose they were changing bennets (bayonets) and striking their guns xc. One of the guns discharged, the ball cut off two of his fingers, passed through the centre of his hand & entered his breast, passing through his body and stoped at his back bone. I saw the Dr take the ball out off his back after he had died. The day was solumn. Our Co went of[f] on picket to guard to stay 4 days. I wrote a let to brother and B F Hine. I did not feel quite so well and did not go on picket. There was a sermon at 3 ½ oclock PM by J B Van Petten. His wife and some other ladies attended. All went off pleasantly but I felt to ill to attend.

At 7PM I conveined under the shade of a large chestnut tree by the road side with a number of others for Prayer meeting. According to notice Mr Van Petten was there to lead the meeting. It was commenced with singing and it raised in interest til two or three would begin to pray at once. This was very encouraging for the first meeting of the kind and the stillness of the evening with the music of tree toads that did not cease to sing in the limbs above us added an additional solemenity to the occasion.

M 2nd I wrote a let for A Warner then I lay in my tent til noon. I talked with Dr Sherman about getting a furlough to go home. The

---

94. William R. Bailey (23) Company H, enlisted at Crown Point.

young man that was shot yesterday was burried at Darnestown in military style,[95] all is pleasant I only wish to feel better.

T 3 There were 4 more negroes crossed the river last night and were taken by our picket. This makes 11 that have crossed and are in our Regt.[96] I feel worse. I have a fevor and lay in my tent the most of the day. At guard mounting there was a fellow come near geting shot. After his gun had been inspected he came to an order arms, and his peice discharged. The ram rod cut his nose and forehead slightly, so the play goes.

W 4 I am feeling much better this morning. I bought a cooked chicken= 25 other things pie xc = 10. I dug a host of sassafras. News come that the enemy were throughing bom shells[97] at our picket opposite the great falls. Our Regt were supplied with new caterages (cartridges) and called away there, a distance of 8 miles; so we have no dress parade. I wrote to C Westman 18 Regt.[98]

Th 5 RM I rested badly last night. I have the direa this morning though I feel very well. I got very cold. There was so much cold rain and had a chill PM. I then felt bad enough. AM I read much in my diary and balanced my money accounts. Found I had spent $18.00 since I left home. I also received a letter from L A Brockett containing a note for $25.00 in return to a check I sent him 13 days ago. Our Co came home from picket on the river. They were very wet.

F 6 I feel feeble. Went to the Dr and got a dose of stimulating drugs. I drew two pairs of socks from the US. There was a pair of shoes, two pairs of drawers, and two shirts due me yet. Two peic-

---

95. No record of this burial can be found in the Darnestown area or with its churches.
96. These "contraband of war" as they were later known, were often allowed to remain in camp to serve the soldiers and assist with camp chores. These were obviously Virginia slaves who crossed the Potomac River when they knew the Federal army was encamped on the Maryland side.
97. Occasional cannon fire from the Confederates across the river.
98. Cornelius Westman (26) enlisted May 1 in the 14th NY Infantry, not the 18th, at Booneville, NY. His association with McLean prior to May, 1861 is not established.

es of canon came to our camp which carried balls 13 lbs weight.[99] There was some heaving firing to the west of us up the potomac. At 6 PM we were roused by the report of the gun and well pleased. Eager for a fight all ready.

S 7th PD I felt much better. AM some more canonading to the west. Our tent was thined out. Mr Comstock[100] & Willie Salisbury was appointed to other tents by the capt. We cleaned our tent and took the floor out then fixed it again.[101] I washed some clothes. It took me 4 hours then I had a fever, felt badly. Am very weak xc. I went out to see the canon and bomsheels & grape in canester. They look dismil.

Sab 8 Cool morning. I was called on guard but the Dr excused me and gave me some powders for two days. There was more canonrading AM though we hear of no battle. Four of us went out to read in the Testament. We enjoyed ourselves in so doing. At 3 o'clock PM our Regt were called into line. We supposed for to hear a sermon, but were ordered to march to the river, dividing the Regt and one part went to the east the other to the west to be ready for a fight. While there was a peice of canon taken to a sightly hill about a mile distant with the intention of storming the enemies camp which lay nearly opposit us among the trees of Virginia. We made quick time and were soon at the dock on the canal which was our destined place. No sooner than we were stationed in the hollow out of sight of the enemy, our men commenced firing and continued an hour and a half without any reply. Then we returned to camp all alive. I felt some soar (sore). I had not been in the ranks for 18 days.

99. These may have been Model 1857 Napoleons, a smoothbore cannon firing 12# round shell and shot.
100. Henry Comstock (42) enlisted May 1 at Graysville, mustered into Company C.
101. It was common for resourceful soldiers to forage lumber to cut and lay a floor in their tents. This comment along with the comment of the two soldiers being reassigned to another tent indicates that the 34th was most likely using large Sibley tents. The Sibley tent was invented by the Federal military officer Henry Hopkins Sibley and patented in 1856. Of conical design, it stands about twelve feet high and eighteen feet in diameter. It can comfortably house about a dozen men.

When we got back we had dress parade. This kept us in the ranks 3 hours. We had a very interesting Prayer meeting under the same old chestnut tree as last sabbath even(ing).

M 9 I drilled a while then got a pass from Capt and went out with H Corp.[102] We got all the peaches we could eat beside the very pleasant walk we had. I had another fevor PM.

[*Editor's Note.* Private John H. Crewell, Company F, found time to write another letter home on September 9. This letter is written on colorful patriotic stationery which depicts the aged General Winfield Scott surrounded by military accoutrements and flags. This stationery was probably sold to John by a local sutler.]

Camp Jackson
Senica Mills
Sept 9, 1861

Dear father
I take the pleasure of writing a few lines to let you know that I am well at present and I hope that when these few lines reach you they will find you the same. I have just received your letter and was glad to hear from you all. The rest of the boys is all well at present. We have got two rifle cannon here with us and we went with one of them down to the canal and threw some bombshells over in Virginia and they said they could see them some. We have got over in Darnestown about fifty thousand soldiers there and there was thirty thousand come there today.[103] There was a boy died in Company I day before yesterday.[104] He died with a fever but what kind I do not know. They had a battle at Fairfax Court House and our folks drove them out of that and they are a ____ then up and their Gen Davis is dead for they have had the flag at

---

102. William H. Corp (27) enlisted May 7 at Norway, mustered in as a Musician in Co C. Later died of disease November 18, 1862 in the U.S. General Hospital, Philadelphia.
103. These troop numbers are likely inaccurate or exaggerated based on rumors among the soldiers.
104. A careful search of the roster of the 34th shows James Cummins (19) of South Pulteney, died of disease on August 20. This is the only death around that time in Company I.

half mast.[105] I don't think the war will last long for they will cave in before long. You said in your letter about what I wrote to in that letter about the officer a goin to the city it was not for our officer alone but for all. What they went to the city for do not know for I did not ask for I thought it was none of my business but I will tell what I did hear that they went to be inspected but that is all. I wrote a letter to _____ but have had no answer yet and he wrote in his letter about the officer but I don't recollect what I said about it. We have had order to keep two days rations on hand for four days. You said you had wrote four letters to me but I hain't received but two from you. I wrote a letter to you last week and I said I should not write again till you write to me. We have not got our pay yet and I don't know when we will get it. And to tell the truth of it our regiment is as corrupt as can be for I feel discouraged for we don't drill enough.[106] We drill only twice a day and they keep us on guard every other day. This is all at present. I shan't write again
From your son
John H Crewell
Write as soon as you get this. Phil has write one to you and one to Jacob Sr with a dollar in for him.]

T 10 PD There was some of our Co called on guard to day. I wrote a let to John Root[107] and one for Fetterly, to my Uncle, I feel first best. Had all the aples I could eat. Drilled at dusk but the Co was called in to go to the river and be ready for a fight if the Rebles should attempt to cross. I did not go but went to a prayer meeting under the tree.

105. There were a few skirmishes in that Northern VA area in late August, 1861, most notably at Ball's Cross Roads, August 27-28 (1-KIA, 1-WIA) and Munson's Hill, August 31 (2-KIA, 2-WIA). Both actions involved the 23 NY Regiment. The CSA General Davis is unidentified further.
106. Crewell does not explain the corruption he mentions but he previously made mention of the drunk officers in the regiment and that may be why he felt they did not drill enough. Obviously, Crewell was serious about his soldiering.
107. John B. Root (18) lived with his parents, two older brothers and one younger sister near Poland, NY. Poland is about 10 miles northwest of Fairfield. The 1860 census shows 21-year-old William McLean living with the Root family.

W 11 I went to wa(t)ch with Wm Burt this M two hours. He was very sick. I lay around the rest of the day. Mr W Corp and another fellow come to our tent and sang til late. We were very much interested & amused. There was rain in the night, our tents leaked. I rolled myself up in my rubber blanket and pined it around me. I awoke in the morning and found myself wet though. We slept well.

Th 12 PD Our Co went off to the fording of the river to be ready incase of an attempt of the enemy to cross, I went along. We were in line at 9 AM ready for march and took a direct line to the R, crossed a draw bridge then trod the toe path two miles down stream and found our stoping place. Had the convenience of a few small brush tents one of which I took a share in. I found a board to ly upon and fixed me a place to my mind. There was corn near and I soon had some roasted coarn. I saw corn stand 15 feet high, the ears so high on the stalk that only a tall man could reach them. After dinner I went to the lock below a few rods and crossed with 3 others. We went toa farm house half a mile back in the fields. There I bought a loaf of bread for 12 cts, then we started to go for peaches. After travelling two miles we found ourselves at our own companys station, but the canal was between us and them, and we were 3 miles from the peach orchard, so we took the nearest way to get back but had to come by the dock and that was a mile. Some of our boys forded accross to the island opposite us and got aples xc. The island was planted to corn. In this way we spent the day and at sunset I find myself writing its adventures xc as I sit on the toe path and listen to the distant sound of canon. I did not rest well.

F 13 PD I went off with Mr Dockstader[108] to get peaches. We went up the toe path to the lock, then to an orchard on a high hill about a mile distant, but when we got there the peaches were all picked. O what a large black snake we saw in the meadow! While going, we found a few scattering ones (peaches), enough to eat, and returned to the lock. Here we got on a boat and rode down the canal nearly to our Co. Then we footed it to them. There was a sight

---

108. Ezra Dockstader (21) enlisted May 1 at Herkimer, mustered in as a Musician in Co. G. He lived with the Emun P. Vorheese family near Newport, NY.

of firing at night. I received a let from Maggie G(ardiner). So the day closed.

S 14 We left our post of duty at ten AM, being releaved by Co K, and had a warm walk to camp. Received a let from M A D (Margaret A Davis) and A Young.[109] All went off well.

Sab 15 WD I was called on guard. This is the first time since the 19th of Aug. I then stood on the same post and caught cold. Was not in the best of tune. Today I feel tip top and strong. I wrote a let to John Gardiner[110] PM and went on guard at 4 oclock. Very warm.

M 16 PD I come off guard at 6 AM & went out at 8. I had the fortune to get a horse to ride out by the guard. A fellow was going out with two and he let me have one of them to ride to the Bridge, as he was going there to water them. I went a mile farther and got milk from a wensh that was milking. I filled my haversack with cucumbers and aples, could not get peaches. There were 3 other fellows in the orchard that I came to camp with. I was weight and = 132. I feel well. There were some very heavy cananading to the east of us at 9 AM. I wrote a let for L Tarble. ~~I sold the wach that bought in Albany for $2.50 for $8.00 to Simon Loyd.~~[111] I received a letter from Amelia Van Slyke at 9 PM. At 10 I was asleep but was roused by the long roll of drums. Soon the Regt were in line and marched to the river. We lay round there till 12. We then learned that the Rebles had fired upon Capt Sponabald and fifteen men that had crossed the R after sunset to Scout and spy. There was thirty shots fired, one of our men killed, two wounded, one of which escaped nixt morning. The ball entered his cheek under his eye. The Rebles took two prisoners beside the wound man & dead body. The rest escaped, some of them in boats & some swam the River.

---

109. Probably Andrew Young (27) from the town of Van Hornsville, NY, which was south of Herkimer and Little Falls. He lived with six other relatives between the ages of 3 and 30 years old.
110. 1860 Federal census identifies 18-year-old Margarett Gordner (sic) residing with her 58-year-old father, John and four other siblings on a farm near the Village of Frankfort in Herkimer County. Correct spelling of her name was Margaret Gardiner.
111. Unknown as to why these lines are struck through. Simon Loyd (21) enlisted May 1 at Fenton, mustered in as a Corporal in Company C. Later wounded at Fair Oaks, VA, May 31, 1862.

This caused considerable excitement in camp, but we returned and rested till morning in suspence.

[*Editor's Note*. This incident is recounted in detail in both the regimental history and *Distant Drums, Herkimer County in the War of the Rebellion*. The regimental history contains Captain Sponable's own words.

> While encamped at Seneca Mills, and being this day, September 16, on duty as regimental officer of the day, Colonel Wm. Ladew told me he had that day heard that a rebel regiment had recently been stationed at Dranesville, a small place, from four to six miles from our camp, the Virginia side of the Potomac. The Colonel relieved me from the duties of the officer of the day, and placed Captain John Beverly on that duty. While I was getting ready to cross the river, Private Oliver P. Darling, of my company, and Bob Gracey, of Company H, obtained permission from the Colonel to accompany me. My instructions from the Colonel were verbal: to obtain all the information possible, and report as soon as practicable; at the time to use my best judgement as to my actions while on said expedition. We crossed the river about sundown, passed into a large cornfield, crossed the marsh on the logs, and proceeded on our way. A short distance behind us came eight or ten members of our regiment, that were stationed at Muddy Branch, on picket, who were on their way to obtain some of the rebels' green corn on the island. Directly after crossing the marsh, as evening was quite light, I proceeded along the edge of a woods on our right, being temporarily shielded on the left by another large cornfield. I took the lead, Darling in the center, and Gracey brought up the rear. The whole of the picket that were following had not crossed over the logs when I heard a slight noise in the cornfield on my left probably not over three rods distant from me. Instantly thereafter I heard the command to fire given, which was followed by a volley of rifles; how many there were I cannot say. I looked over my shoulder and saw both of my companions fall, and, supposing them dead, as my hat had been knocked off my head by a rebel bullet, I thought it time to rejoin my regiment, if possible to do so. In much less time than it takes to tell it, I turned to the right, passed through the woods, and came out about a half mile further up the river than I had crossed earlier in the evening. Upon arriving at the river, it took me but a moment to decide what was best to do: swim the river at once, or remain to be captured. I plunged into the river, and immediately thereafter the rebels commanded

me to return. Not feeling disposed to obey their order, I swam as fast as possible, they at the same time accelerating my exertions by firing about twenty shots at me, none of which, however, hit me, though they came in rather close proximity. Upon regaining the camp, I found the regiment under arms, and also learned that some of the shots fired at me had entered the camp. Bob Gracey was taken prisoner but subsequently escaped by drugging his guard. On his return to the regiment he told me that, while a prisoner, he paid an Irishman two dollars to bury two men, he supposing that I had also been killed, as was Darling.

An unnamed officer in Company C later wrote,

> I got Company C in a position that commanded the river for a mile or two. I then learned that Captain Sponable and all his men had either been killed, or taken prisoners. I started to go down to the river crosslots, when whom should I meet but Sponable himself, with only one boot on, and wrapped up in a big shawl. Lost one boot, leggings, and revolver in swimming the river. I was overjoyed to see him, but could not help laughing at his ridiculous appearance.

According to the account of the incident in *Distant Drums, Herkimer County in the War of the Rebellion*, Captain Sponable understated the situation. While Sponable's account is a detailed first-hand account, Distant Drums provides some additional information. This account says that reports vary as to whether Sponable was acting with or without orders and that he blundered "into an ambush by three rebel companies, who unleashed a 'perfect volley'." Quoting from *Distant Drums*,

> The sound of gunfire roused the camp of the 34th and in a short time the men lined the riverbank scanning the water for signs of Sponable's squad. Eventually a boat was sighted and as it approached the bank the men forlornly noted that there was only one man on board. On landing, Pvt. William Graves (Company D) of Champlain told a sad story, he was the only survivor as all the rest of the party had been killed outright or mortally wounded. Throughout the rest of the night and into the next day eight more survivors from Sponable's scouting party swam the Potomac and staggered back to camp. Only two of the men were actually wounded, but all of them were thoroughly soaked and furious at Private Graves for taking their only boat (presumably the one in

which they crossed). Wells Sponable, minus a boot, his hat and his revolver, had floated across in a swamped rowboat. Henry Bramley and Christian Zaugg of Company D were the two wounded men, the former slightly and the latter seriously, a ball having passed through his cheek. Zaugg, who received a medal from the Pope and had participated in the charge of the Light Brigade, or so he said, had escaped capture by lying in a pond all night with just his mouth and nostrils above the water's surface.]

Of the three men who had not returned, Oliver Darling of Salisbury had been killed and Robert Gracey and Cyrus Kellogg of Crown Point had been taken prisoner. Gracey, who was also seriously wounded, would recover and escape back to the 34th within a month. The date of his return to the regiment is unknown but the *Herkimer County Journal* reported on October 24 that Gracey had drugged his captors using the opium he had been given for his wound and escaped. The regimental history states that when Gracey returned, it looked like he had "a hard time and indeed he had. It appears that he had been shot through and through, the bullet entering his chest, passing through one lung, and out his back. 'Big Bob' was surrounded by the comrades, and had to tell the story of his adventures many times over during the days that followed." As a consequence of his wound, Gracey was discharged from the service a year later. Kellogg was held prisoner for eleven months until his parole in August, 1862. *Dyer's Compendium* shows the September 16th skirmish in their listing for Maryland activities as occurring at Seneca Creek and involving a detachment of the 34th NY. CSA units involved are not identified.

Putting both accounts together provides a truer picture of the seriousness of the incident. Had the Confederates been more accurate in what was probably also their initial engagement, losses to the 34th could have been substantial. This type of discretionary order was to plague the Corps of Observation prior to the Battle of Ball's Bluff on October 21 which resulted in a massive defeat for the Federal forces and the death of Lincoln's dear friend and Oregon Senator Edward D. Baker. Congress subsequently created the Committee on the Conduct of the War.

Another brief account of the incident was written in a letter by 26-year-old Sergeant Samuel Shell, Company B, on Friday, September 20. The letter was written to 25-year-old Miss Adeline Tubbs in Herkimer, New York. Sgt. Shell's spelling and punctuation are very poor. Periods have been added for clarity otherwise the letter is transcribed as written.

Friday September 20 1861
Camp Jackson
Sineca Mills
34 Regt N.Y.S.V.

Miss Adelian Tubs

You must excuse me for not ritin to you befor for i hav not time to rite to you for I hav bin very bisey and i have now laisure time to spair. So i thought i wud right a fiew lines to you that i am well at present and i hope that you are the same. we have good times down here. we ar about 26 miles from washington. it is a very good plais war we are in camped near in sight of virginia shor. Some of our boys was over their last nite and the rebb picket fired on the boys and killed won of them and wonded one and took for prisoners. the won that got wonded in the chase got a way from them. Som of them got back to the boat and went off for the other shore and some swam the river and with the rest the Capton came Swiming a Long for shor. You coud here the rebles holler ketch the devils as they ran threw the corn field. They thought the Capton was dead but he turned up all rite. ther was an awful huraw than for som time after his return back to camp. i don't think that thir is a nuff of them in virginia to tak him a prisonor.

adelin i wish that you was her with us. yo wood see grat times her. yo wood not wantto go back to little Falls agan. We have all kinds of a musing our Selv. som plays cards and Som Singin and some ____ing and some dancing. Som rasting for there work is lazy. they wood git dam lazy that they wood not mov. i must now cloas my leter. ther is won thing yet. wen you git married to mark you must let me now so i can com to see you maried.

So far well. i must go on garg for it is 7 oclock and i hav two ours to stand. So good nite. i cant rite more to nite.

yours respectfull
Samuel Shell M.D.
Miss Adelin Tubs
giv my best respek to All my inquiren frends.

On October 17, J.B. Van Petten wrote to the Utica Morning Herald about the incident which occurred a month earlier.

The Affair of the Scouts of the 34th Regiment.
Darnestown, Md., Oct. 17.
In a previous communication was narrated the fact of a party of eleven scouts from the N. Y. 34th having crossed the river, and being attacked and cut to pieces by a superior number of rebels, The particulars of the affair are thus detailed by Corporal Robert Gracey, of the party, who until his return on Monday was supposed to have been dead.

On the night of the 16th of September, a detachment of twelve men crossed the river for the purpose of reconnoitering [sic[and foraging. When reaching about half a mile from the river they were attacked by fifteen rebels, two of whom were instantly killed. Among the wounded was my informant, Corporal Gracey of Company H, a man of gigantic frame and iron endurance. As Gracey lay wounded upon the ground, a rebel named McCarthy Lowe, a farmer residing in the vicinity, rushed up and shot him twice, both barrels taking effect, and was stopped from firing a third time by his Captain.

One of the balls entered Gracey's back in a slanting direction, and came out on his left side, the other entering his back lodged in his left lung, where it still remains.
His two weeks stay at Fairfax was not of an unpleasant character, considering all the circumstances.

In this hospital the inmates were mostly members of the 1st Virginia regiment. Every day or two those seriously ill were sent to Richmond, as it was feared that General McClellan would attack the rebel lines.

During Gracey's confinement his sufferings were intense, as evinced by a comparison of his former with his present weight. His attendants furnished him with opium every night, but he treasured it up as a means of his ultimate escape. One night after he became able to move about, he drugged the beverage of his attendants, and left the hospital in pursuit of cold water for a violent tooth ache. After passing the outer guard he fell in with the sentinels of three distinct lines outside the village. He was repeatedly hailed, and fired at three times, but all the balls failed to hit him. He started towards the Potomac, at the point of his capture, but in consequence of large rebel forces he was compelled to diverge in a westerly direction, crossing Bull's Run, and thence taking a circuitous route to avoid observation. After three days of hunger and suffering he reached the Potomac.

While in the hospital at Fairfax, Gracey had opportunities of becoming familiar with many important facts. He occasionally overheard conversations between officers and the surgeons of the hospital.

On the 5th inst., Jeff. Davis was at Fairfax, and spent several hours with Beauregard. Gen. Johnston was understood to be somewhere in that neighborhood, but Gracey did not see him. On one occasion Gen. Longstreet said to the surgeon, that the rebel forces in front of Washington were so scattered that if attacked at any point on the line, there must be an abrupt retreat by all upon Manassas, our Gibraltar. They think it impossible to be driven from this point. It was generally believed that Beauregard would burn the village of Fairfax Court House if compelled to evacuate it. It was impossible to ascertain the exact number of rebel troops in and around Fairfax. They were variously estimated from 50,000 to 100,000. As far as Gracey's observations went, they were better fed than clothed, but he heard of no complaints in regard to the latter, although their uniforms presented a curious mixture, gray predominating over other shades. Salt ha'd been scarce, but the supply was becoming more plentiful. He learned that hundreds of men were employed on the sea shore in evaporating, each man producing on an average two bushels per day. It was also coming in freely from the western part of the State.

On his homeward route Gracey saw, about one-fourth of a mile northwest of Fairfax, a breastwork about thirty rods long and five feet high, but no troops were then stationed there. He saw no large bodies of troops north of the Great Falls, but lay concealed until forty baggage wagons passed toward Leesburg.

Private George H. Denny (27) was a member of the First Company, Howitzer Battalion (AKA Richmond Howitzers Light Artillery) which was formed in Richmond, VA, and mustered in on April 21, 1861, for one year. On September 25, 1861, he penned a letter to a close friend at the Union Theological Seminary in Hampden-Sydney, VA. In the letter he describes some of the latest action on the Virginia side of the river. He writes from a camp near Leesburg "at Whites Spring".

> The Howitzers to which I am attached are near Leesburg on the Potomac guarding a Ferry which it is thought the Federals may attempt to cross. We have a brigade here under Genl Evans numbering about 3500 men....we have received orders to keep ourselves in readiness to march on a moments warning & if they come over we are to contest every inch of ground even if against fearful odds.

We are now within gun shot of the enemy and can see them easily but they are on the Maryland side of the Potomac and behind their fortifications so that we can not do them much harm even should we open fire on them. We had a small skirmish with them resulting in the death of one of our number and one wounded. The loss of the Federals must have been considerable as we opened upon them with our battery throwing shell right into their ranks. Their (minnie) balls whistled over our heads like hail. We have two prisoners taken on this side of the river by the Mississippi regt. They will be sent south.]

17 We were marched to the river this M to lay in readyness for the skirmishers if they should return & fire upon our canons which threw a voley of boms into Virginia. There was a rapid fire from our gun for an hour, but we received no reply. Therefore stoped and went back to camp without any satisfaction. I wrote a let to Amelia Van Slyke. We had a shower at 3PM.
W 18 I did the police duty with Chas Powers[112] & wrote a let to L A Brocket. The paymaster of the Reg't came, all went off well.

[*Editor's Note.* Along the Potomac the soldiers of both sides were in close proximity to one another. Because of this, there was frequent interaction between the soldiers on patrol on both sides of the river. They frequently talked and exchanged news with one another. They wanted to know each other's regiment. When possible they met in mid-river to exchange newspapers, tobacco, coffee, and other sundries the other side did not have. Such activities were discouraged by the officers however they could not prevent these interchanges and meetings.

Additionally, there were instances of shelling, primarily initiated from the Federal side to the Confederate side. The Confederates did not always answer as they were spread more thinly than the Union troops. The Federal soldiers also crossed the river to conduct reconnaissance and determine troop strength on the other side. All of these activities were written about by the 34th's Chaplain, John B. Van Petten, in his report to the Utica Morning Herald on September 18, 1861. The actions described in this report preceded the Battle of Ball's Bluff by a month and indicated increasingly activity by the troops on each side towards their foes.

112. Charles L. Powers (29) enlisted May 1 at Russia, NY. Mustered into Company C.

From the Upper Potomac.
DAWSONVILLE, Md., Sept. 18.

There has been no serious demonstration on the part of the rebels within the past forty-eight hours, and as far as can be learned, everything along the upper Potomac remains in a state of quiet to-night.

The Division Quartermaster to-day protested in the name of the War Department, against the payment in coin of any bills for damages sustained by owners of property where encampments are located, but he will certify to such claims based on principles of equity, leaving it to Congress or the Court of Claims to authorize the payment.

The cause of this procedure is supposed to have arisen from the fact that most of the Federal coin heretofore disbursed for this purpose, has found its way to the secession side. It is understood that supplies for forage and subsistence are not included in this protest.

Yesterday an unauthorized scouting party of the 34th New York Regiment went across the Potomac, near the mouth of the Seneca, and were attacked by a superior party of the enemy. One of our men was killed, and several wounded. One of the latter was shot through the cheek, but fled, pursued by the attacking party. On reaching a creek he threw in his gun and plunged in himself, laying on his back and resting his head upon a stone, with his mouth and nostrils above the water. He evaded his pursuers, and after three hours submersion he crawled to the shore. His companions who were on the Maryland side, discovered and rescued him while making a vain attempt to swim across. These incursions, which can be productive of no good to our cause, are condemned by experienced officers.

The 2nd Rhode Island battery, stationed near the mouth of the Seneca, yesterday shelled an encampment of the rebels nearly opposite, and it is believed that several were killed. The enemy did not respond, probably from want of artillery.

It is reported that a Lieutenant and several men belonging to one of the river guard regiments crossed the river secretly, and is believed to have deserted to the rebels. The name of the officer and the regiment are withheld until the report can be verified, but the authority is conceded to be reliable.

Our own and the enemy's pickets are said to frequently meet on one or the other shore of the Potomac and pass the time in social intercourse, occasionally partaking of each other's hospitality.

This morning at daylight it was discovered by General Stone's pickets, near Conrad's ferry, that the enemy during the previous night had commenced and partially constructed an entrenchment on the Virginia side, about 500 feet from the shore, upon a slope facing the river.—One of our light batteries opened upon it about, nine o'clock, and after twenty or thirty rounds, nothing was to be seen of the enemy, and little results of their labors.

For some days past conversations have been held between our own and rebel pickets, from which it has been discovered that the latter belong to the 2d Richmond cavalry, "who were anxious to exchange late Richmond papers for the leading Union journals, but our pickets declined to reciprocate.

Lieutenant Colonel Seward, nephew of Hon. Wm. H. Seward, Secretary of State, recently from serious indisposition, withdrew from the command of the 19th regiment and proceeded to Washington, when he tendered his resignation. But before it was accepted, a rumor reached him that a battle between a superior force of the enemy and the division to which he was attached was imminent, and notwithstanding his physical debility, he withdrew the resignation, and immediately re-joined his regiment.

There is great complaint in regard to mail facilities in this division of the army. Numerous letters never arrive, while others are days and weeks behind their time. This is attributed to local officers and carriers, rather than to the Department at Washington.]

Th 19 We were payed the first thing in the morning $23.66 which was pay for two months. We have received now for the soldiering $45.72 which is the privates wages since the first of May. Our Co went off on picket on the R. I went to the end of the pickets up the river which is 4 miles. We found some lice in the shanty which was at our station. I set fire to it and there was straw enough on it to make a splendid blaze. It raised to the limbs of a high tree and we thought it was going to burn us out of a home. I killed a black snake on the toe path, 4 feet in leingth. Then crossed the canal on a raft and threw accross some rails to build another shanty off. We worked hard a(nd) got up a good rak to sleep in. I think we were tired, only three of us to work: Daniel Embody,[113] L Tarble and my-

---

113. Daniel A. Embody (20) enlisted May 1 at Norway, NY, mustered into Company C, later promoted to Corporal.

self. I am writing. The other boys are eating supper and the sun is about to go down. I went on centry at 7 PM and was more lonesome then I ever was while on guard. The evening was very clear, a full moon and very still. Not even a breeze passed through the trees to brake the silence. The singing of the tree toads and locusts add to the occasion a solumn aspect, while the screech of the owl and the unsatisfied bark of the desturbed dog in the distance indicated that something was out of place. Still further the continual droping of acorns from the trees above me helped to make the scene spookish and dreary.

F 20 I went to Camp and had a ride two miles on a canal boat. Then I went to a negroes and got what milk I could drink. I then went to Peters orchard and filled my haversack full of aples. I stade in camp till two oclock, saw a Co payed, got two loves of bread and started back to picket. I felt rather tired when I got back.

[*Editor's Note*. A very detailed 1865 Martenet and Bond map of Montgomery County, Maryland shows at least six Peters families living in the vicinity where Seneca Creek enters the Potomac River, any one of which could be the location of the orchard. This point is adjacent to Pennifield Lock on the C&O Canal. Pennifield Lock was the 22nd lock on the canal, counting from Georgetown, DC, 20 miles distant. The lock was completed in May, 1831, at a cost of approximately $10,000. This is location is also just west of Rowser's Ford, a popular crossing point for Confederate troops entering Maryland. In 1985, Charles T. Jacobs added color elements of US and Confederate routes of travel, crossings and camps to this map. He identifies two Union camps in the vicinity; one just east of Seneca Creek and the Potomac River and one along the road to Darnestown on the Thomas Magruder farm. Another camp is depicted at Darnestown. Unfortunately, the units at each of these camps are unidentified. The distance from the Seneca Creek camp to Darnestown is just over two miles and would have been easily walked from any of the camps.]

S 21 W.D. We lay in our shanty till noon. I shot accross the canal at a litter of pigs and missed them, and put a mark on the other side of the river. After dinner we were releived by another Co. We had a long march coming to camp, 5 miles. I received a let from Simpson and Benie and a paper from F Smith.[114] Some rain PM.

114. There are several possibilities of a Frank, Frances, or Francis Smith in Herkimer County.

Sab 22 Quite cold. I am on guard again. PM I wrote a let to father respecting Simpson's coming to inlist in our Co.[115] There were rebles seen accross the R laying up batteries. At 3 oclock our gun was taken to a hill in sight where they threw a few shells to the rascals to commence with. They (Ed. meaning their own soldiers) spoiled one of our canans by having a shell burst in it,[116] then the music of the large guns ceased til sunset. Then our men opened fire on the rebles again with another gun. To all of our shooting there was no reply but some running. We could see the rebles run for their lives. I bought potatoes, 20 cts. We received a countersign and purole for the first time we have had both. The countersign was Elaxandria and the purrole was Elsworth.[117] No one was allowed to pass out of camp without giving both of these though any one could pass in by giving the countersign. Mr Jacob Ashly[118] came into our tent in the evening and we told stories. I never had time pass more pleasant then when I was on guard. Mr Hogan and I stood together and we related some of our naughty acts when we were boys. Moonlight and cool.

M 23 I wrote a let to L A Brockett and put 25 dollars in it, to risk by mail (it was in US Treasury notes). I had a good breakfast of potatoes and butter P.M. I sold my Wach for $8.00 to Cyrus Eldridge[119] and took his note till next payday. The Wach I bought in Albany for $2.50. I was sleepy and slept the remainder of PM. There was a

115. Simpson McLean did not join his brother but enlisted as a Private in Company F, 29th Ohio Infantry on November 1, 1861. His enlistment papers incorrectly list his age as 18. He was actually 16 years old.
116. The bursting of a shell inside a cannon tube was not unusual, especially with inexperienced troops as these men were. Various reasons, including defective ammunition, could account for the accident and the cannon may or may not be repairable.
117. An obvious reference to the death of Colonel Elmer Ellsworth in Alexandria, VA, on May 24th. This incident was certainly still fresh in the minds of the men of the regiment.
118. Jacob J. Ashley (30) enlisted May 1 at Graysville and was mustered into Co C as a Sergeant. Ashley was killed at Antietam September 17, 1862.
119. Cyrus Eldridge (24) enlisted May 1 at Graysville, mustered into Co C.

number of orders read at dress parade concerning picket duty and marching from one place to another without music xc. Three boys of company B went off Saturday I suppose they run away. Martin Zimmerman was in the Co.[120] I wrote some at dark.

T 24 W.D. I passed the guard at 8 AM with an old pass that was <u>not dated</u> and went through the woods till I was out of sight of the camp. I then took the road to Darnestown. I had the company of a felow from the 2nd Mass Regt who had been under guard at Washington and was now on his way to his Regt. I had some fears of being asked for my pass by the guards at D(arnestown) but was not intoragated by them at all. I made a purchase of .375 in paper

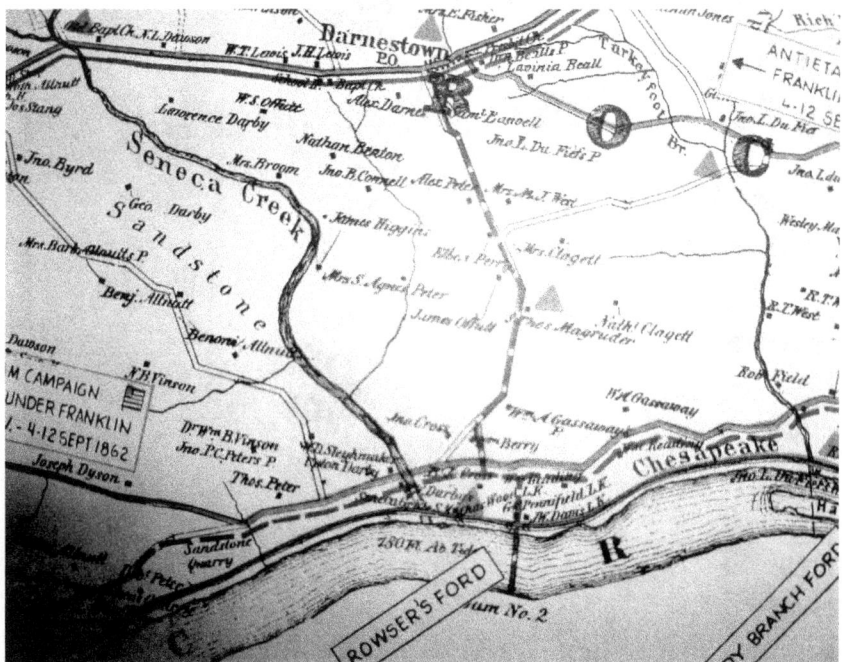

The vertical dotted line in the center of the map is the road from Camp Jackson to Darnestown. (Source: Library of Congress).

120. McLean mentioned talking with Zimmerman on June 25. Perhaps desertion was on his mind at that time. The regimental history confirms Zimmerman's desertion date.

Darnestown in 1861. "To River Road" on top left is the road south going to the C&O Canal and the Potomac River. (Source: Library of Congress).

and sacars (cigars).[121] I then started for camp but had gone but a few rods when I met a serjant of our Regt and 8 men. I was halted and asked for my pass; then (the sergeant) added there have been no passes given to any of our men to day and we are sent to arrest all we see out of the lines. I gave him my pass and my name. He then told me I must fall into the ranks and go back into the town with them. I refused till I saw that to refuse was only foly. I then fell into the Squad and went back. There was 3 or 4 guards over me till noon. I was then left in the store in care of 2 while the rest went to eat dinner. I wached the movements of my guard. Soon one of the(m) lay down in the stoop and the other set by him, there being quite a crowd in and around the store. The most attentive guard that was over me was interested and his atention was called to the movements of the gang. I wached my chance and when his head was turned from me I slyly took my paper and sacars and sliped out of the door, jumped off of the platform and took a double quick half way to camp. I was not noticed so I escaped without detection. I met 2 fellows on the road & was afraid of them but I took (to) the fields a short distance and passed them. I urging my way on to camp soon found that I was at the path which I left when I came out of the woods. I returned on it again and come to a spring and passed the guard. I sold all the paper and envelopes that I had and some sacars. I felt afraid of being taken but was not, though the squad came back and gave my name. While I stood in line the Corprel of the guard at dress parade the corprel of the guard came to me and asked me if I had been out, and said that there was a pass entered to the officer of the guard with my name on. I made a strange thing of it and said that it was not possible that any pass was given in my name. This was the last of it.

W 25 I went to the lock with the officer of the guard to help arrest the pickets there which were drunk. We brought all of them but one that was dead drunk and lug upstairs in his own pis. O! how far below the beast many are that wear the human form. I went with the other fellows a mile down the toe path to the nixt lock then we came to camp. I lay round, wrote some. Evening spent story telling.

121. This purchase could have been at Samuel Fisher's store and Post Office. See location on Darnstown map above.

Th 26 I called on guard and came on the the 3rd relief and had not to go on til 2 PM. I wrote a letter to Robert Hoselitt,[122] sold some sicars xc. C Willoughby[123] talked of going home on a furlough on the account of his foot. When I went on guard I read and wrote all the time. I received a letter from J.B. Root.[124] I packed my letters to send by C. Willoughby to Fairfield. He expected to go home but did not get his furlough signed by some means. I was on guard in the rain 2 hours, from 2 till 4 night. I was rather sleepy and the guard for relief came close to me before I saw them. The sergent did not give me the countersign. I was not detected.

F 27th DD I sold some sicars, examined 2 heads, wrote a letter to B F Hine. A heavy wind, leaves are falling. I did not come off of guard till 10 AM. There was no dress parade.

S 28 I changed the date of an old pass and went out on it with Mr H Greenly. We had all the milk we wanted for dinner by going 2 miles for it. We then searched for aples and after a tegeous (sic. tedious) tramp we suckceeded in getting our haversacks full of aples from trees that had been shaken. We came back at 3 ½ PM and sold our aples for 19 cent each. We then went out on the same pass with some washing to a darky woman.[125] Then attended dress

122. Robert Hazlett (20) years old as of the June, 1860, Federal census, lived in Frankfort, NY, with his parents, a younger brother and two younger sisters. He labored on the family farm with his father who was also a blacksmith. Frankfort is 16 miles from Fairfield and just northwest of Ilion, NY. Perhaps Robert had been in school at Fairfield Academy.
123. Charles A. Willoughby (18) enlisted May 1 at Norway, mustered into Company C. Wounded at Antietam, he was discharged six months later from a hospital at Baltimore, MD.
124. This is the family with whom William was living at the time of his enlistment. They were on a farm near Poland, NY.
125. Quite a few blacks came into camp with the 34th at Seneca Mills. The regimental history mentions Addison Phillips, his wife Nellie, and a small infant. "Nellie established a laundry at Camp Jackson, and did quite a thriving business." Addison was a free man as he "is living at the Falls, and did own several houses and lots there. See Chapter XI, Post-War Years, for additional information regarding Addison Phillips.

P. This even is very cold. We felt cold with our over coats on. I got a dose of medicine from the Dr this morning. Had some pain in my bowels last night.

Sab 29 I cleaned up my gun, took the things out of my napsack and was busy all the AM. We had a sermon at 10 AM. I then wrote a let to Magie Gardiner and was busy examing 6 heads the rest of the day and evening = 1.50. Slept cold.

M 30 I am on guard. Our orders are not to sit down while on our posts, and keep up our guns from resting on the ground, no smoking nor unnecery talking. There was heavy canonading at 9 AM & at 10 about 5 miles down the R at the Great Falls. Some of our men were wounded but they made the enemy retreat.[126] I wrote a let to Ad (Andy) Van Slyke then I had a slight chill of the ague,[127] but I kept up and did my guard duty. The night was very cold, and I cought some if I may judge by my feelings. So ends the month of Sept.

[Editor's Note. The incident on September 30 is corroborated and detailed in a letter written Private Isaac G. Campbell, Company G, who was detailed to Great Falls on July 31 along with Companies B and I. In writing to his sister on Tuesday, October 1, he related,

> It is all War-War-War. The rebels riddled the buildings all to pieces that (we) were quartered in at the Great Falls. They commenced firing about daylight on Sunday morning and threw 10 solid shot but no shell. One man on our side had his gun bent almost double by a shot while (in his) hands. One side of his face has turned black. He was the only one hurt. If they had shelled them, it would have been a different affair. The cowardly traitors retreated as soon as our battery came in sight. The rebels directed their course up the river. We expected to get some shot from them this morning. Shot is (of) no account by the side of shell when fired into an encampment. We could have returned their compliment with shot or shell from our brass beauties but it is now noon and we have seen no sign of the sneaks. I guess they won't trouble

---

126. This action at or near Great Falls is not noted in *Dyer's Compendium* or in the regimental history.
127. Ague is a 19th century medical term describing a fever marked by chills and sweating; also a fit of shivering.

us for they have had a taste of our shell and found them full of meat-but not of the sweetest. We have had one man killed, 2 men wounded and 4 taken prisoners by the rebels. They were scouting on the Virginia side when wounded and taken."]

October 1861

T 1st Our Co were sent on picket. I was stationed near the stone quarry. I went off to a negroes and got two canteens filled with milk after returning to picket which was a mile. I went half a mile down the toe path and got bacon that I had left there, then I crossed the canal and went back to the negroes and traded off the bacon for butter. I came to my post and had a chill of the ague again, I lay by the fire till 7 PM, but eat no supper, but went on guard at 9 and wached the river two hours. I never was on so pleasant a post. We could see up and down the river each way three miles. All went off pleasantly. The countersign was Nepolien. The purrole, Saint Helene.[128] We had a shanty to sleep in so I rested the rest of the night.

W 2 Very still morning. I wrote some and then went to the negroes and got a canteen full of milk. There was some rain. I had a hard chill, lay in the shanty and took a sweet. Did not go on guard till the fifth releif at 3 in the morning. There was some cananading AM down the river. Some of our men left the Regt to become cavelry men. There was five taken from each Company.[129]

Th 3 I went to the negroes and got milk and butter again, then came back and fixed my thing to go to camp as we are to be releived today. There was heavy rain west last Sunday and the river raised 6 feet so many of the picket were obliged to leive or move their shanties from the bank to higher elevations. After I came to camp I had another chill then went (I got a let from R Northrup) out on dress parade.

128. St. Helena is the island in the South Atlantic Ocean to which Napoleon I was exiled by the British in October, 1815. He died there in May, 1821.
129. Men from the 34th Infantry were transferred into the cavalry at several different dates during this time. Notes in the regimental history indicate that the transfer was into the US Cavalry rather than into a State cavalry regiment.

F 4 I wrote a let to R Northrup, sent for my wach. I got one from L A Brockett with an answer to the $25 I sent him the 23rd. Bought a revolver = 1.00, than ran some balls and felt well.

S 5 I wrote to L A Brockett, then went out to wash some clothes. Then I fired off my revolver, picked up some (undetermined word) and then came to camp and wrote some xc xc. Then took up another diary to write in.

[*Editor's Note.* At this point the daily diary entries for William McLean's first diary end. The next page was left blank. On the page following the blank page, William records the "names of those I wrote to: Father, Brother, Uncle, Bernie Hine, James Moody, Amos Willoughby, John Root, Cornealious Westman, John Davis, Leonard A Brockett, John Gardener, Robert Hazelett, Hiram B Ellis, Robert Barr, Anderson Young, Nelson Carpenter, Jasper Lawton, Andy Van Slyke."

William leaves a blank line, then adds the names of the women to whom he wrote: "Magie Gardiner, Amelia Van Slyke, Rosena Northrup, Mary A Davis, Gertrude Carpenter."

On the following page he makes the notation:

September 6th 1861
I drew two pairs of socks there is two shirts a pair of shoes two pairs of drawers due me yet (I drew shoes).

The inside back cover contains a largely illegible list of items bought by William and what he paid for them. The initial entry is for something bought at Albany. It may be this diary. He paid $1.93 for a coat and likeness. This may be his reference to having his picture made in Albany. Shortly after he paid $2.00 for a watch. He mentions various items bought from a sutler. One readable reference is to a "shirt and hat at Camp Jackson $3.00." He also lists the $25.00 he sent to L. A. Brockett. The next entry appears to be additional money he sent to Mr. Brockett. In the next few entries, William totaled the money he spent during the duration of this diary. His meticulousness in recording these purchases and uses of his money is unique among diarists. McLean obviously wanted to keep close track of the use of his meager funds earned from his military service. Perhaps he did the same in subsequent diaries.

This ends the first diary of William C. McLean.]

Chapter IX

The Affair at Edwards Ferry

On October 6, 1861, William McLean says he began his second diary, further documenting his service with the 34th. Within a few days, the situation for the 34th was going to rapidly heat up, culminating in their first engagement with the enemy at Edwards Ferry.

The observations and occasional scouting parties across the Potomac River and along the lengthy portion of the river for which the 34th was responsible were designed to gauge the movements and strength of the enemy. This part of the upper Potomac had numerous fords and ferries used by farmers before the conflict in both Maryland and Virginia to transport goods down the Chesapeake and Ohio Canal to the markets of Georgetown and Washington City as well as to trade across the river in Leesburg, VA, and Poolesville, MD. In fact, two ferries, which were very active before the war began, existed in this area. Conrad's Ferry (now White's Ferry and still in operation) was opposite Poolesville on the north side of Harrison's Island. Six miles south and not far removed from the southern tip of Harrison's Island was Edwards Ferry. Harrison's Island was privately owned and its very fertile soil was actively farmed. A few houses, barns, and outbuildings existed on the island. A few miles north of Conrad's Ferry towards the mouth of the Monocacy River was White's Ford, a frequent crossing place which was used by both sides throughout the war.

Much of the trade from the Virginia side was stopped in April, 1861, but families on each side of the river had relatives and friends on the other side. Crossings that were previously numerous before the war had virtually ceased but there was still clandestine communication back and forth both by signaling and actual passing of letters and other correspondence by those who crossed over. Such communication was of concern to the Union command as sentiments in this part of Maryland were sharply divided and commanders worried about Confederate sympathizers and spies in Maryland conveying information about Federal troop strength and movements to their counterparts across the river in Virginia. It was against this backdrop and with this paranoia that the Union command was to encourage the actions which led to the Battle of Ball's Bluff, the engagement at Edwards Ferry, and the formation of the congressional investigation and Joint Commission on the Conduct of the War.

The purpose of this work is not to deal with the debacle at Ball's Bluff as that subject has been thoroughly covered by other authors. However, the 34th New York contributed to the Union action at Edwards Ferry which occurred three miles south of Ball's Bluff. As this was their first significant encounter with the Confederate forces, it is noteworthy in the experience of William McLean and the history of the 34th New York Infantry Regiment.

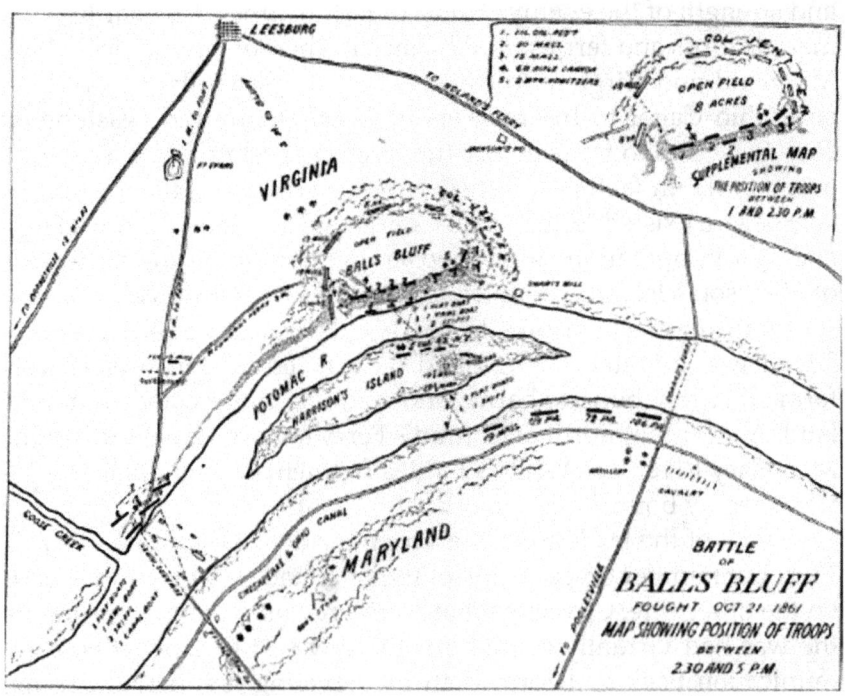

Lower left corner: Edwards Ferry; to the right of Harrison's Island: Conrad's Ferry. (Source: Google Images).

The 34th remained in place at their Seneca Mills base until Monday morning October 21, the date of the Ball's Bluff battle. On this morning they received orders to march to Poolesville, MD, a distance of about eight miles. Poolesville was a sleepy little town about three miles removed from the river. In command of the regiment was Colonel William LaDew.[130] They would march up the canal and turn right on one of the roads leading from the river to Poolesville. It would be a pleasant walk on a beautiful autumn morning. About two miles into their march their destination was changed to Edwards Ferry which was closer than Poolesville and along their line of march.[131] During their march the apprehension and concern of the men was heightened as they heard distant firing in front of them. They had to be asking each other what was to lie ahead on this day.

The regiment arrived at Edwards Ferry about noon, joining other troops who preceded them to the ferry. Troops had begun to cross before their arrival and they had to wait their turn. They learned that two other regiments had already crossed. They surmised they were in for a fight as they listened to the heavy cannonading from the Union batteries against the rebel positions on the Virginia side.[132]

Crossing the river would be a slow laborious process as written by Louis Chapin,[133] the author of the regimental history. "The means of transportation to the western bank of the river were nothing to brag of. Two old scows had been conscripted from the adjacent Chesapeake and Ohio Canal, and we were poled back and forth in primitive fashion. During the afternoon our turn came, and for the first time the regiment squatted on the sacred soil of old Virginia."[134] The first companies to cross were I, E, and G according to First Sergeant Henry Lyon of Company I. William McLean's

---

130. William LaDew was 33 years old and from Gray, NY. He enrolled in Albany on May 30 and was mustered in as Colonel on June 15. He resigned from the regiment March 20, 1862.
131. *Distant Drums*, page 16.
132. *History of the 34th N.Y.S.V.*, page 25.
133. Louis Chapin was a 19-year-old private from Little Falls who enlisted May 1.
134. *Distant Drums*, page 16.

General Stone's Division at Edwards Ferry, October 20, 1861
(Source: *Harper's Weekly*)

turn was to come later. The men watching the first crossings had to be concerned about their method of transport across the river. Lyon reported in a letter to his family dated November 7 that "we accordingly loaded ourselves in an old flat-boat and set sail. The sail in question being poles in the hands of 5 or 6 men. But as the rate of locomotion was slow we did finally reach the other side at the expense of much poling as the Current was very swift. But we made port in the mouth of Goose Creek and anchored our noble barge."[135]

Pickets were thrown out to their front with the balance of the troops massed near the river on the flood plain. The minor movement of the 34th while on the Virginia side was noted by Sergeant Lyon, "We were marched up from the river a few rods, drawn up in line, told to stack arms including Knapsacks and hold ourselves in

---

135. *Desolating This Fair Country*, edited by Emily Radigan, 1999, page 46.

Goose Creek entering the Potomac River. (Source: Author's collection).

Edwards Ferry looking across to Goose Creek. Goose Creek is the opening in the trees to the right of center. (Source: Author's collection).

readiness for anything that might present itself."[136] The men continued to hear the artillery and heavy musket firing a few miles away from them, but no orders came. The afternoon proved uneventful for the infantry regiments, cavalry, artillery, and sharpshooters who had crossed over. Unknown to these troops, the Confederates who had been in the area near them were called to join the desperate fight a few miles upriver at Ball's Bluff.

Since the advent of the Congressional Joint Committee on the Conduct of the War on December 9, 1861, various theories have been offered to explain the horrendous debacle at Ball's Bluff. In fact, the US Congress created the Committee to search for answers for the disaster and to assign blame. Ultimately, the responsibility for the tragedy was assigned to the deceased Colonel Edward D. Baker, who of course was no longer around to defend himself. However, one of his former soldiers in the 71st Pennsylvania Volunteers, John D. Baltz, a private in Company H who was present at Ball's Bluff, published a book in 1888 defending Colonel Baker's actions in an attempt to exonerate him.

Many mistakes were made on October 20-21, 1861, by the Federals. What stands out first and foremost is communications in general and the lack of clarity and specificity in the issuance of orders in particular. It was very early in the war and communications techniques were still being refined. The fact remains that there were several thousand Federal troops a short march away at Edwards Ferry who were generally idle while the battle was going on upriver. In his 1888 book, John Baltz, a detractor of General Stone, wrote, "We will now leave General Stone (who was in overall command of the troops in the Edwards Ferry and Ball's Bluff region) reposing on his laurels at Edwards Ferry, busily engaged in explaining his movements so as to relieve himself from all blame, hence his first report contained many straws which subsequently sank beneath him. We will notice here but one of the many statements in that re-

---

136. *A Little Short of Boats*, page 118. Henry C. Lyon was 24 years old from South Pulteney, NY and had mustered in May 22. He was later to die of wounds received at Antietam September 17, 1862.

port, 'one thousand men (would have been) enough to have turned the scale in our favor,' which must have been a consoling thought to Stone, when mindful of the fact that he had about four thousand men and two pieces of artillery within two and a half miles of the battle-field, idly listening to the whole engagement, to whom he gave no orders to advance and engage the enemy, although they were in good condition and eager for the fray."

There was no direct communication between the troops at Edwards Ferry and those at Ball's Bluff. Keeping within Union controlled territory, such communication would have been difficult and time consuming with the messenger having to cross from Virginia to Maryland, travel up the C&O Canal towpath two to three miles, cross the Potomac River from Maryland to Harrison's Island, then across to Ball's Bluff to deliver any message of Federal reinforcements coming from the south to assist at Ball's Bluff. Had such action been undertaken, the Confederates would have had to divide their forces and fight on two fronts, perhaps allowing the Federals to gain the advantage. As General Stone later explained in his testimony on January 5, 1862 before the Joint Committee, such coordination and a fight on two fronts was not his intent. "These troops on the left (Edwards Ferry) were held in readiness to be thrown at once on their retreat, in case Colonel Baker had fallen upon a small force, and pressed them off; they were held here so as to dash across and cut off the retreat of the enemy on the roads." Thus, the troops at Edwards Ferry remained idle, bored, foraging for their next meal, and listening to the sounds of the battle just to their north while their comrades in arms were leaving their blood on the field, in the woods, and in the Potomac River.

The afternoon and evening were to pass uneventfully for the 34th. Boredom and wonderment likely consumed them. The last unit to cross over from Maryland was the 7th Michigan. By this time rumors began filtering into the men about the disaster which was occurring a few miles upriver. The 7th Michigan was ordered to entrench and build rifle pits and breastworks at the top of a ridge above the river and on both sides of the Edwards Ferry Road which coursed to Leesburg, a few miles away. The 34th continued to watch and wait. They were in the vicinity of a farm of the Dailey family who had a substantial amount of livestock. Bored and hungry soldiers looked to the Dailey livestock for food and activity. Fence rails provided the cook fires. Sergeant Lyon noted in his diary, "then began to look around for something eatable which we soon discovered running around in the shape of Pigs, Cattle, etc. We soon tamed a few of them and commenced some tall eating. We took Care of ourselves as more than fifty hogs and about twenty cattle can testify."[137] One might wonder after such a banquet in what fighting shape these men were!

Confusion seemed to reign as the Union troops were later told to cross the river back to the safety of the Maryland side. Sergeant Lyon recalled that the 34th began crossing the river only to be told upon arrival on the Maryland shore that reinforcements were coming and we were to return to Virginia. Return they did. Reinforcements did come during the night and into the next morning of October 22. Two additional regiments, two companies of two other regiments, and 80-100 additional cavalry added to those already occupying the hilltop rifle pits beyond the river.[138]

October 22 dawned rainy and miserable. While the cold Union troops waited and wondered what was to come next, 13th Mississippi troops under Colonel William Barksdale moved from their victory at Ball's Bluff and occupied the woods between the Dailey House and Kephart's Mill along Goose Creek. It was late in the afternoon before Barksdale's 600 men surprised the Federals. A very short but sharp skirmish ensued which resulted in small losses on both sides as the Confederates were driven back by the advanced Union infantry and batteries. The units in advance of the 34th bore the brunt of the engagement. Louis Chapin, in the regimental history, mentions that "Company G was thrown forward to support the pickets, and the rest of the regiment held in reserve." The 34th was not specifically engaged though some may have anxiously discharged their weapons. Accordingly, there were no casualties in the 34th. The Mississippians did not attack again that night or the next day and the 34th "made a Capital retreat under cover of darkess"[139] the night of October 23. Louis Chapin noted that "Captain Wells

---

137. *A Little Short of Boats*, page 118.
138. *A Little Short of Boats*, page 187.
139. *Desolating This Fair Country*, page 49.

The Affair at Edwards Ferry

Artillery firing in support of Union troops on the Virginia side of the Potomac River at Edwards' Ferry, 22 October 1861 (Library of Congress)

Sponable of Company B, and Private James Faville[140] of Company K, were the last persons to leave the Virginia side. Coming to the river bank, they found large numbers of muskets, and a great quantity of provisions, abandoned on the bank. All this stuff they threw into the river before leaving."[141]

There was watchful waiting on the Confederate side as they thought the Federals were massing for another attempt. But it was not to be. Henry Lyon of the 34th continued his letter on November 8th, "The next morning the baffled enemy came down and found nothing but our deserted ground looking far worse than it did the day we Crossed. They vented their indignation by calling our pickets on this side Cowards and telling what they would have done if we had staid a few hours longer. The wind was blowing furiously which rendered it unsafe to cross at all that day but kept up a show of Crossing and parading his forces back and forth over the hills making the rebels believe that large forces were continually arriving and Crossing. The thing turned out very well for us for if they had come down on us Wednesday in all probability the affair at Ball's Bluff would have been repeated and few of us would have been left to tell the tale."[142]

140. James Faville (39) enlisted at Salisbury May 1. He survived his two year enlistment and mustered out with the regiment.
141. *History of the 34th N.Y.S.V.*, page 27.
142. *Desolating This Fair Country*, page 49.

The following image, gleaned from Harper's Weekly a few weeks after the Edwards Ferry affair, shows how history becomes distorted and carried forward for generations. The image incorrectly shows the troops retreating across the wide Potomac on a "canal boat bridge." This is woefully inaccurate. There was no canal boat bridge and the troops had to make their slow and laborious retreat in the same hazardous manner in which they originally crossed; a few small boats against a very swiftly moving current. Later, in June 1863, a pontoon bridge was constructed at Edwards Ferry for the use of troops crossing on their way to Gettysburg.

Retreat of Union forces to the Maryland shore at Edwards' Ferry, night of 23–24 October 1861 (Library of Congress)

With their service at Edwards Ferry concluded, the 34th marched to Poolesville and settled into winter quarters at their new camp, named Camp McClellan after the beloved Union commander. They were encamped with several of the regiments who were engaged at Ball's Bluff. The campfire conversations and their letters home over the next several weeks certainly told the story of their near encounter with the disaster at Ball's Bluff.

Chapter X

Correcting the Official Records

William McLean initially applied for an invalid pension in September, 1879. That pension was granted and he began collecting the normal monthly pension amount as allowed by law. For an unknown reason, after receiving a pension for 33 years and at 72 years of age in 1912, William realized that he was not getting the full amount to which he felt he was entitled. Thus began his correspondence with the Commissioner of Pensions in Washington, DC, to correct this error. Perhaps the error was discovered by his attorney who kept him abreast of changes in the law which increased the pension amounts. In his first letter written to correct the error, he suggests that perhaps the error was made by the notary who originally filed his claim. Thus begins a series of letters with the Pension Bureau. The letters from the Bureau revealed to William previously unknown and astonishing information about his service records which surprised him greatly. Given his lifelong attention to detail, William would make every effort to correct this unfortunate injustice. Had this error not been discovered, the blemish on William's record would have remained forever. Only he could right this wrong.

    Utica Oct 25 1912

    Mr J L Devenport
    Commissioner of Pensions
    Dear Sir
    My Certificate No 189419 reissue is incorrect. I enroled April 20 1861 in Co C 34th NY Infantry was discharged at Albany June 30th 1863 with the Regt expiration of service. I was drawing $15 a month for 2½ years age pension. If John

Evans (Notary) who filled my claim made any mistake in age or service I would like to correct it. I am rated $21½ should be 23. Will you please have this made right.
Resp Yours, William J McLean
318 Neilson St Utica NY

In this response from the Bureau of Pensions to William's first letter of inquiry about the monetary shortage in his pension amount, William learns for the first time that he was absent without proper authority; in effect, deserted. Upon reading this letter, William was incredulous! It was now up to him to prove how this break in service occurred and to attempt to correct this mistake and his pension amount.

>Department of the Interior
>Bureau of Pensions
>Washington
>
>Removal Division
>Inv. Ctf 189419
>William J. McLean
>Co. C 34 N.Y. Inf.
>November 23, 1912
>Mr. William J. McLean
>318 Neilson Street,
>Utica, N.Y.

Sir:

In response to your communications of October 2, and 25, 1912, received October 4, and 28, relative to your above cited claim for Pension under the Act of May 11, 1912, based on age and length of service, you are advised that a careful examination of the evidence in the case, shows that no error was made in the rate of $21.50 allowed. A report from the records of the War Department shows that you enlisted June 15, 1861 and were discharged June 30, 1863, and that *you were absent without proper authority two months and twenty five days* (italics added), making your actual pensionable

service one year, nine months and twenty one days, and your age alleged is seventy two years.
Very respectfully,
(signed) J L Davenport
Commissioner

Immediately upon receipt of the reply from the Pension Bureau, William set about writing back to correct his record. His memory was still very sharp in recalling the details which led to the error in his record. Perhaps he had recorded this very specific information in previous years but that does not seem plausible given that his first inquiry into the deficiency in his amount was in 1912.

> Utica Dec 2 1912
> Mr J L Devenport
> Dear Sir I feel a deep gratitude for you & your department for the careful search you have made in my case. I will try to explain. I was wounded see Dec 13 1862 at Fredricksburg at 5 PM. Next morning the 14th I was taken accross the river to the falmath side where a tent hospitable was being prepaired for the wounded. About dusk of the 15 over a thousand of the wounded were taken away by train & transfered to a boat on the Potomac & landed at Point Lookout on the 16 Dec 1862. While I was at this hospitle my meals were served in the ward as I was wounded in the foot. Each man had a card on the head of his couch giving name birth place fathers name & mothers maiden name. My card gave my birthplace Philadelphia Pa. The state of Pa sent a commission of Drs who with the surgeon in charge of the Hospital examined all the Pa boys wounded at Fredricksburg with a view to have them transfered to their own state. My name by mistake was reported by the ward master among the Pa troops & I was was examined with the others. 200 names were sent up to Washington to get consent of removal.
>
> Page 2
> 40 were accepted and I was one of them to my great pleasure Before the list of names were returned from Washing-

ton the ward master had discovered his mistake and said to me as I wasn't a Pa Soldier. I couldent be transfered to the state if accepted. We had some hot words and I told him if I didn't go he wouldent be ward master. I was not interfeared with (and) left Point Lookout Feb 13 1863 and went to Turners Lane Hospital Philadelphia Pa arrived there Feb 15th 1863. Was sent later March 14th to Washington & Alexandria arrived at Alexandria March 18 1863. All these 3 months I was coresponding with my Capt & Lieutenants (Tho[mas] Corcoran RL Gorman & Wm Wallace & a number of my comrades). I was never a deserter or away from comand a day without leave But the ward master at Point Lookout to cover up his mistake reported me deserted or missing. While at Alexandria Va I rec(eived) a letter from James Todd fi[r]st Sergt of my Co telling me I had been reported to the Co deserted. I showed the letter to the ward Dr & he told me to write to the surgeon in charge at Point Lookout and get a statment of the date of entry and transfer. Also to Turners Lane Philadelphia & he said he would give me a statement from Convalesant Camp Alexandria when I left there. I went to my regiment with these three papers & gave them to my Capt & never have heard a word from it since till your letter came over.

Page 3

When discharged I received my full pay & 100 Dollars bounty. Also $50 dollars bounty March 10th 1868 by act of July 28th 1867. These statements are stamped on my discharge by the paymaster. I have never thought for a moment that there was on the records any blot against me. I feel it does me a foul & cruel injustice. This is or should be vindicated by the public records of the Hospitals. It does seem if such things are recorded against a person wrongfully that the proof of the falsity should be recorded as well.

My Dear Mr Devenport Will you please see if there is not a vindication of this blot or what can I do to have it corrected. *I wrote a diary every day I was in the army & from it I have these dates at the end of 50 years.* (italics added)

With regards & best wishes
I'm T C & L William J McLean

Two and a half months later and probably upon the advice of an attorney or other person familiar with such procedures, William wrote to the Adjutant General of the United States. In this lengthy letter, William very clearly and graphically spelled out exactly what happened with him after his wounding at the first Battle of Fredericksburg. All of these minute facts were most likely contained in another of his diaries. Certainly, it would have been difficult, if not impossible, to recall such facts after more than 50 years. William kept the diaries, cherished them, and they became his salvation in this disputed situation.

Utica NY Feb 15th 1913

Adjutant Gen US
My Dear Sir
I have just been informed by our commissioner of pensions that I am reported absent from my regt without leave from March 14th 1863 to June 9th 1863. *Dear Sir I can give an account of myself every day from May 6th 1861 when we (our regt) went to Albany NY to drill until the 30th day of June 1863. I have a written diary of every day.*[143] I was wounded at Fredricksburg Dec 13th 1862. On the morning of the 14th I was taken in an ambulance across the river to a Hospital camp they were puting up near Falmath. The afternoon of the 15th I & a 1000 others were loaded on the RR cars and run to Aquia creek at Bell plains & loaded into boats & sailed up the Chesapeake bay to Point Lookout Gen Hospital which we entered Dec 16th. On the 27th day of June 1863 this Hospt was visited by a commissioner from Pennsylvania who wanted their state troops who were wounded at Fredrickburg transferred to their own state. My birth place was given on the card that each of us had at the head of our

---

143. Italics added. William is adamant about proving his case.

couch as Philadelphia, the Wardmaster got mixed at this & gave in my name as a Penn soldier. These names with a description of their wounds was sent to Washington DC for approval. 40 names were accepted from the 200 that went in & mine was among them. I was wounded in the foot & had 7 small slivers of bone picked out of it

No 2

(by the) Dr at differant times. My meals were served me in the ward while I was there. I was in no way to blame in having my name mixed in where it dident belong. But I was very anxious for the change. Philadelphia had been my home & I had many friends there. While those names were hinging at Washington my Wardmaster learned his mistake & came to me & told me I had no right to go & he would have to hold me back. We had some very hot words (I think he feared me). However he dident try to prevent my going. He gave me a pass card as he did to the rest in his ward which was taken up by the guard at the gang plank as we entered the steamer. To cover up his mistake, when the boat had gone he reported me missing. This was Feb 13th 1863 & I entered Turners Lane Gen Hospt.

[*Editor's Note*. Turner's Lane Hospital, sometimes referred to as the "German" Hospital was located at Twentieth and Norris Streets in North Philadelphia, west of Broad Street. The Union Army rented it from the German Hospital of Philadelphia from 1862-1866. Sources list the hospital as either a 275 or 400 bed facility. Turner's Lane Hospital was the first hospital in the United States devoted exclusively to neurological injuries, especially those related to amputations, and soldiers with "nervous" disorders. These patients, in later wars, might be diagnosed with "shell shock" or post-traumatic stress disorder. The work of physicians at Turner's Lane Military Hospital stimulated interest in neurology in the United States, leading to the post-Civil War emergence of neurology as a distinct medical specialty. These physicians advanced their profession and benefitted their patients. Because so many of the patients lost limbs, Turner's Lane was dubbed "Stump Hospital." It was the most famous of Civil War-era research hospitals. Susan Ritter Trautwine McManus (1841-1881), a young German immigrant, was a caregiver at Turners Lane Hospital and a diarist who recorded the details and struggles of the patients she saw.

The fact that William McLean lost a toe and had sections of bone removed from his foot may be the reason he was selected to be sent to Turners Lane Hospital. The hospital was a new US hospital at the time McLean was sent there.]

Sabbath morning the 15th I was sent to Washington the March 14th 1863 was there a day or two & sent to convelacent camp Alexandria the morning of March 18. I was in this camp till about the first of June. I was given a pass & sent to the soldiers retreat in Washington to awate the coming home of my Regt 34th NY. I havent got these dates as one of my little diaries has been miss placed. All the time I was away I had a weekly corespondence with some one in my Co at the front. I wrote to the Capt Thomas Corcoran[144] & RL Gorman,[145] Lieu(Louis?) & Gen Gormans son Lieu,[146] Wm R Wallace,[147] DA Embody,[148] CA Wiloughby,[149] (and) 1st Sergt James Todd[150] who wrote me while at Alexandria that I had been reported to the Regt a deserter. I showed this

144. Thomas Corcoran (23) enrolled at Graysville and mustered in as a Captain in Company C; a position he held throughout the war. Corcoran died at the Soldier's Home in Milwaukee, WI, January 21, 1903.
145. Richard L. Gorman enlisted in St. Paul, MN April 27, 1861 as a private in the 1st MN but was discharged for promotion as a First Lieutenant into Co C of the 34th January 1, 1862. He was promoted to Captain in June, 1862, later resigned March 2, 1863. Richard originally served under his father, Willis, a Colonel in the 1st MN. Willis Gorman later became a brigadier general.
146. This would be another son of General Willis A. Gorman, probably Louis or Lewis.
147. William R. Wallace (23) enlisted May 1, 1861 at Graysville. He was mustered in as First Sergeant, Co C June 15, 1861.
148. Daniel A. Embody (20) enlisted at Norway May 1, 1861. He was promoted to corporal and mustered out with the regiment. In 1903 he was living in Auburn, NY.
149. Charles A. Willoughby (18) enlisted May 1, 1861 at Norway. He was wounded at Antietam and discharged in March, 1863, as a result of those wounds. In 1903 he was living in Hannibal, MO.
150. James H. Todd (23) enlisted May 1, 1861 at Fairfield with William McLean. He served his full term and mustered out with the regiment.

letter to my ward Dr & he told me to write to Point Lookout to the Surgeon in charge & to Turners Lane Pa & get their certificates of my

No 3
(date) of entrence & transfer & he said he would furnish me one so I would be all right. I met my regt at Washington armed with these papers & our Co & Regt rolls were made out for full pay & I supposed I was all right on the books of the war department & never have known any different until I got my pension certificate for the time increase. Its a cruel & unfair injustice to me to have this false showing on the war record. If there is any records of these Hospitals in Washington they will show that my statement is true. I was actualy in the servace two years & two months from May 1st till June 15 1861 the state paid us in gold 11$ a month. We were at Albany drilling every day & sworn into the US service the 15 of June & discharged at Albany June 30 1863. Dear Sir (I don't know your name). I hope that your department will look up this matter & have it corrected as I have been informed you have the right & power to do. *My writen diary would convince you or any Court or jury of its truthfulness* (italics added) & you can have it to examin if you want it.

I remain Respectfully your
William J McLean
Co C 34th NY Vol Regt

Less than ten days after William penned his letter to the Adjutant General, his case was investigated and a response forwarded to the Commissioner of Pensions. Given the time it took for the mail to reach its destination in Washington, be opened, and assigned to an investigator, such a quick response to the Pension Department is most remarkable. The fact that this letter also found its way into William's pension file at the National Archives is also significant. William's claim was promptly investigated and his assertion was proved correct. William challenged the official records through the use of the information in his diaries and he was vindicated, at least in the eyes of the War Department.

> War Department
> The Adjutant General's Office
> Washington
>
> February 24, 1913
>
> Respectfully forwarded to the Commissioner of Pensions
>
> Upon a further examination of the official records in connection with the allegations made herein it has been ascertained that the charge of desertion in March, 1863, standing against William J. McLean, Company C, 34th New York Infantry, is erroneous, and that it does not appear that he was absent without authority at any time between that date and June 9, 1863.
>
> (signed) Geo. Andrews
> The Adjutant General

Unfortunately, while the Adjutant General was now believed William, the Commissioner of Pensions was still not satisfied. He requested additional information of William and posed a "problem hard to solve." His letter to William did not exist in William's file and it could not be located elsewhere. What can be assumed is that questions posed by the Commissioner caused William to relate family history going back to his birth in Philadelphia. Fortunately for the modern reader, this abbreviated family history permits us to better understand the McLean family and its wanderings. Whether requested or not, William took the further step of having this letter notarized. He even went so far as to indicate that he was a Lincoln man in the election of 1861; a comment meant to enhance his case.

Utica NY April 12 1913

J L Davenport Commissioner

Dear Sir
Your favor of April 3rd is at hand. You have sent me a problem hard to solve. I will tell you what I know about this & testify to every word I write. I was often told by my parents that I was baptised into the Episcopal church in my infancy. I don't know what town or County this church was located in. My parents had a family bible with the dates of birth & I saw the date of my birth there often which was Jan 15 1840. The book I believe was made in England & about the first of the last century as I remember it. It was about 7 inches long 5 inches wide and 3 inches thick bound in black plain leather. My mother died in Feb 1852 or 3 & father married again & there are 4 children of the 2nd family living. I dont know where some of them are. My father died in 1893 & I then asked my stepmother for the old family bible & she claimed that she didnt know where it was & I asked her oldest daughter that was married if she had it & she didnt have it & I cant recolect having seen the old book in over half a century. My father was a mover he moved elevan times between 1846 & 1858. This is all from memory. First we lived in the county on a farm then in Philadelph city where he was a gingam weaver & then in N York state & in different towns & Co there & *in Feb 1858 he went to the state of Ohio and lived near Painsville. I dident go to Ohio with the family. I stayed in NY so as to attend the schools as I had & I studied & taught till Sumpter fell & then I went to the front from Fairfield acadamey Herkimer Co NY.*[151] *& my father & brother enlisted in the 29 Ohio Regt in 1861*[152] (italics added) & my brother was

---

151. This explains why William was in Fairfield attending school and living with a local family.
152. This was the definitive letter that proved the identity of the diarist. John C. McLean and Simpson McLean both enlisted in Company F, 29th Ohio Infantry; John on September 18 and Simpson on November 1. Simpson was the previously unidentified person mentioned in the diary.

5 years and one and a half months younger than I. I was a few months too young to cast my first vote for Lincoln but I voted at Norway Herkimer Co the next March at town election 1861 & have voted every year since except while in service in the army.

 State of New York   William J McLean
 County of Oneida

 Subcribed and sworn to before me this 15th day of April 1913
 Robert Bailey Jr
 Notary Public

The above letter ended any controversy or question that still existed pertinent to William's case. His pension file contains nothing more. William challenged the Federal records and was successful. He surely felt very proud and even ecstatic at his victory. His service record was now complete and accurate for all future generations and for the readers of his first diary to enjoy.

Since the original military service records are not corrected or amended with the information provided by William, the reader of only the military records will come away reading that William was a deserter when, in fact, he was not. The lesson for researchers is that they should be diligent in checking both military and pension records and not just rely on the military records for correctness.

Chapter XI

The Post-War Years of the McLean Family

William J. McLean

Precious little is known about the life and history of William immediately after the war except what can be gleaned from the Federal census records and other sources. It is likely that, at least for a while, he returned to his teaching position at Fairfield Academy. If his family had not yet moved back to Herkimer County from the Painesville, OH, area, William could have returned to take up temporary residence again with the Root family until he could establish a place of his own. William developed quite a relationship with Margaret Gardner as they often wrote to each other during the term of William's service as he noted in his first diary. Their wartime writing relationship blossomed into a romance after William returned. Six months after his return, William and Margaret were married on December 30, 1863. Margaret was 20 and William was 23 years old. It appears they resided in Fairfield through their early married years. That is where they were living in June 1865 per the New York state census. They lived in a small frame house valued at $200 and had a 27-year-old "servant" girl, Hannah Wood, living with them.

Margaret Jane Gardner was born in 1843 in Ballymena, Antrim, Northern Ireland, to John Gardner and Margaret Jane Rossborough. She was named after her mother. Margaret's mother died in 1847 in Ireland, perhaps in childbirth with Margaret's sister Agnes or shortly thereafter. In about 1853, John Gardner and his five children emigrated to the United States and settled near the village of Frankfort in Herkimer County, New York. John took up farming with his oldest son, John Jr.

The first child of William and Margaret, daughter Jennie (also named Tennie A. in the 1865 NY State census), was born on Christmas Day, 1864. Unfortunately she was destined for a short life as she died at the age of three years and three months on March 10, 1868. Margaret was six months pregnant with William Jr. at the time of Jennie's passing.

According to the June 16, 1870 Federal census, 30-year-old William and his 28-year-old wife, Margaret, were living and farming near the Village of Stratford in Fulton County, NY. Fulton County is directly east of Herkimer County. Today Stratford actually straddles both counties. At this point, they had two children; Gertrude (4) and William Jr. (2). Gertrude was born July 14, 1866. William Jr. was born two years later June 19, 1868. William had a rather prosperous farm valued at $5,000 and personal property valued at $2,000. By this time, William's parents, John and Sarah lived next door to them on a small farm. (See biography of John C. McLean in Chapter II and this chapter for additional information on the John McLean family.) William continued to work and to father additional children. Another source identified a daughter, Margaret L, who was born on June 11, 1870 but was not recorded on the 1870 census. James C. was born March 5, 1872; Clayton S. was born August 17, 1875; and Bessie M. was born October 9, 1878. This made seven children born to William and Margaret. Unfortunately, James lived a short two and a half years, passing away on August 4, 1874. Three months later Margaret was pregnant with Clayton.

William did not file for a soldier's pension until September 19, 1879. At that point he filed for an Invalid Pension. William was 39 years old and still married to Margaret. His application said that since the war he had resided in Herkimer and Fulton counties. Fulton County is adjacent to Herkimer County so William did not stray far from his original home base. He lists his occupation as a farmer but states that prior to the war he had been both a farmer and a teacher. In his declaration he claims that he is "half disabled" from his war-related wounding. The bone of the toe next to his little toe of his left foot was removed as were other slivers of bone. This injury continued to cause him stiffness and pain. A subsequent examination by a surgeon in Little Falls in April, 1881, assessed his disability at "one quarter or two dollars per month". William was continuing to try to gain additional pension consideration for in

December, 1886, he filed an affidavit stating that he is afflicted with "chronic diarrhea" since his time in camp at Seneca Mills and Camp Jackson, MD, in August and September, 1861. He even names the two regimental physicians who were treating him. Indeed, William has diary entries during this time period to substantiate his claim! This small amount of pension income was to assist in sustaining William and his family for many years to come.

The 1880s proved to be both tragic and memorable for the William McLean family. In early June of 1880 he and Margaret were still living in or near the village of Stratford. Their home was the 15th visited on the census taken June 2nd so he may have been living in close proximity to the center of the village. William was now 39 and Margaret was 36. Curiously, the census shows a nine-year-old daughter, Leona M. This is the same person as Margaret L. who went unrecorded on the 1870 census. The year 1882 was a tragic one for William. His first love, Margaret died on March 31, leaving William to care for 5 children under the age of 17. William and Margaret had been married just over 18 years. She was 39 years old. Margaret is buried in the New Forest Cemetery in Utica. Fortunately, the three eldest children were old enough to be of help with their younger siblings. William was engaged in more than farming for the census notes his occupation as a "farm insurance agent". Perhaps he was forced to turn to a different job to provide for his family or the insurance agent position was in addition to his farming.

William applied for a pension for his wartime service but the pension was not immediately granted. He was examined by surgeons several times in 1880 and 1881 in connection with his pension application. His war wound from the Battle of Fredericksburg was well documented during those examinations. His permanent disability was listed as "one quarter". At this time, such a disability was worth an additional two dollars per month. William was about average size for the time and an otherwise healthy man. At age 40 he was documented as 5'8", weighing 140#, with a pulse of 76, and respiration of 18. William continued to seek additional disability as evidenced by the affidavits and surgeon's certificates for 1886 and 1887 in his pension file. He was now seeking compensation for chronic diarrhea contracted in August and September, 1861. Apparently he was successful, for by early 1890 William was receiving $12 per month.

As was customary in those days, William took another wife less than two years after Margaret's passing. He married Sarah Maria Kimball on November 7, 1883. Sarah was eight years his junior, born March 10, 1848 in Frankfort, Herkimer County, NY. Sarah took over the motherly duties as stepmother to the children. During the balance of the decade, two daughters were born to William and Sarah. Nettie Agnes entered the world on Christmas Day, 1884, and her sister Sarah Eugenia followed almost five years later on November 17, 1889. It's possible that during this decade several of the older and now grown children left the home.

It is unfortunate the 1890 Federal census records were lost in a January 10, 1921 fire in the basement of the Commerce Department Building in Washington, DC, before they were committed to microfilm thus leaving gaps in the William McLean family history. The few details known during this decade are gleaned from various records available primarily through Ancestry.com. An 1890 Veterans Schedule, which notes McLean's service in the 34th New York, lists his address as 66 Neilson Street, Utica. This Schedule shows his enlistment date as April 20, 1861, the same as stated in one of his letters to the Pension Bureau. His official records in the National Archives state he was enrolled May 1 at Albany. William wrote his intention to enlist on April 20 but did not actually get enrolled in the regiment until May 1. He did, however, leave Fairfield on May 6th per his diary. His military records show his muster out date as June 30, 1863 at Albany while the Veterans Schedule shows his discharge date as July 3, 1863. The enlistment date of April 20 is correct. Note the difference in terms between "enlist" and "enroll" and between "muster out" and "discharge". It's possible that several days passed between the actual muster out date and the recorded date of discharge; so both of these dates are considered correct. This is another reason to carefully read all of the terms printed on military and pension records.

The Utica city directories for 1891 through 1895 show William J. Mclean residing at 126 Neilson Street. His occupation is abbreviated as "com. trav." which may denote commercial traveler (i.e. a traveling salesman). After 11 years of marriage, Sarah McLean passed away on December 24, 1894 at Utica, and at the young age of 46. Today she lays at rest in the same cemetery as Margaret. William had a hard time taking care of the two young girls by himself because it is known from a deposition given in 1924 by his daughter Nettie, that William placed the two sisters in an "orphan asylum".

William was destined to marry yet a third time. Eighteen months after Sarah's passing, William married Hannah Fosmire on June 2, 1896. He and Hannah were married at North Broadalbin, NY, which is Hannah's home area. Hannah resided on a 35 acre farm in the house in which she was born in 1848. North Broadalbin is 36 miles east of Stratford, on the shores of the Great Sacandaga Lake, and still within Fulton County. It is not known how William knew Hannah but she may have been a friend of Sarah. This was the first marriage for Hannah and the third for William. There was nine years difference in their ages. William claimed his daughters from the orphan asylum and brought them to North Broadalbin to live.

Unfortunately, this marriage was not destined to be a happy one or to last. William's relationship with his two previous wives, his physical and perhaps even mental afflictions from his war service, and his 84-year-old father-in-law (Jacob Fosmire) living with them in Broadalbin, all contributed to the downfall of the marriage. In 1900, Nettie Agnes was now 15 and Sarah Eugenia was nine. The family lived on the farm together for four years until William moved back to Utica. Nettie returned to Utica with her father while Eugenia, who was in school at North Broadalbin, remained living there with her stepmother, Hannah.

William's pension steadily grew as various increases were passed by the US Congress. Commencing February 25, 1910, his rate was increased to $15 per month based on an act passed February 6, 1907. William was following or was kept abreast of pension developments for on May 18, 1912, he again filed a declaration for pension based on an act of May 11 of that year. He still listed his occupation as a farmer but he now resided at 318 Neilson Street in Utica. His pension rate was subsequently increased to $21.50 per month. In this application, submitted September 16, 1912, the Federal records have him only serving one year, nine months and twenty-one days with a deduction for an "absence without proper authority". This is the notation that caught William's attention. Up to this time, he was unaware of his break in service according to the records. Now this break was costing William a portion of his pension benefit. Thus, with his first letter to the Commissioner of Pensions dated October 25, 1912, he began his extensive and detailed letter writing campaign to have his record corrected. The correction of his records gave him a pension increase to $23 back to May 20, 1912.

Trouble in the marriage of William and Hannah began quite early. According to an information questionnaire William completed for the pension office dated March 12, 1915, William states that "We haven't lived together since 1900. (They married in June, 1896) She has a farm at Broadalbin & I won't live there & she won't live with me here." (318 Neilson Street, Utica). Based on this questionnaire, his pension increased again to $30 commencing January 15, 1915. Subsequent increases brought William's pension to $50 per month, which it remained until of his death. Although they never divorced, William and Hannah continued to live separately. After a three week illness, on Monday, February 27, 1922, William quietly passed away at 6:30 a.m. at his home in Utica. William is buried on a beautiful hillside in the New Forest Cemetery, Utica, NY. A Masonic emblem decorates the top of his large gravestone. Also engraved on the same stone are the names his first and second wives and two of his eight children. It is presumed they are buried with him.

A year after William's death and with the help of William's son, William G. McLean, Hannah wrote a letter dated February 8, 1923 to the Pension Bureau seeking a widow's pension. Her letter was passed on to the law department of the bureau on February 14th. Hannah stated that, "I was parted from my husband at the time of his death, not a divorce but he just went away." For obvious reasons, she did not initially reveal that they had been "parted" for 22 years! After a series of letters between Hannah and the Pension Bureau and submission of their marriage certificate along William's death certificate, Hannah's request was successful. She was granted a widow's pension of $30 per month commencing March 7, 1923, by an accrued pension order issued July 11, 1924. Her pension was later increased to $40 per month. While the marriage of Hannah and William was not successful, her seeking of his pension after his death certainly was. Hannah stated in her later communications that they separated between 1900 and 1903.

A deposition given by Hannah McLean on June 26, 1924 sheds considerable light on their relationship and troubles. She states, "He lived with me here seven or eight years, I guess it was…I don't know the exact year he returned there (Utica)." She goes on to say, "My husband visited me here two or three times after he returned to Utica. After we had been married only a year or two he moved his things back to Utica, but he moved them back here again. He went there in the fall and came back here the next spring. He did not move his things away again until he went back for good. He visited me here two or three times after he had moved his things back for good and stayed a day or two at a time. He drove here with a horse. One of those times he hoed the garden for me. Yes, he stayed over night with me at each of those times. It was too far to drive back the same day."

Of their relationship, Hannah stated, "He did not appear to be angry at all at those times, but he was angry when he first went away. He had been mean to my father and to me and we did not agree very well. I did not order him away, but he went away angry. The last time I ever saw him was probably 17 or 18 years ago (circa 1906) and that was here at the house. No, I did not attend his funeral. I did not know of his death until I saw it in a newspaper. No, I was never in Utica after he left me, but I was there with him before that on a visit." Hannah goes on to talk about a bill of separation that was drawn up by an attorney, Clarence Smith, in Johnstown, NY, and signed by both parties. She claimed she never had a copy of the bill and that it was kept by the attorney.

Hannah was 75 years old at the time of the deposition was taken. She was living alone and was in need of the pension money. She was visited quite a few times by William's daughters, Nettie and Eugenia. Hannah's brother, James, lived with her for seven years after William left, but he passed a year earlier. She states her other brother, John, was with her last summer. These relatives were helping maintain the farm. The New York State census of June 1, 1925, shows that she was living alone on Thyne Road. No such road is depicted on current area maps. This was probably the same residence Hannah had always known. By 1930, Hannah was still living but unable to live alone. The Federal census records her as living with 33-year-old William H. Rose. This record shows Hannah as an aunt to the single William Rose. The Rose surname remains unexplained though it could be the married surname of a sister to Hannah. Records checks have been unsuccessful in determining this family connection. Hannah passed away on October 20, 1931, at Broadalbin, NY. Hannah outlived William by more than nine years.

Additional information on the McLean family is provided by a deposition given by Nettie A. McLean on June 28, 1924 at Utica in regard to her stepmother's widow's pension application. This deposition is the source of information of William placing the two sisters in an orphan asylum after the death of their mother, Sarah. Nettie states that, "one year after he returned here (Utica) he returned to Hannah and stayed a year or so with her and then he came back here to our old home where he lived until his death". In regard to their separation, Nettie stated, "There were never any divorce proceedings. He wanted her to come here and live in our home in Utica, but her father stood in her way. She would not come away and leave him there. My father objected to supporting her out there, and he in here, so they drew some sort of a bill of separation, but they never divorced". Nettie goes on to say that her father's death certificate shows him a widower. She says, "we had it put in that way because we did not want it aired around that he left a widow who was not living with him". She also states she has no interest in the pension claim and that Hannah should have the pension. "I have nothing against it or her. She helped to bring my sister Eugenia and me up and she was always good to us." So ends the sad story of the last years of William J. McLean. In the end, however, he was still able to provide for his family.

Simpson McLean

At some point after his arrival home, Simpson, his father, and the entire family packed up their belongings and moved back to Herkimer County, New York. There was nothing to hold the family in Ohio. This move would bring the family back to a familiar area and a reunion with William and his family. It is reasonable to assume that Simpson moved back to Herkimer County with his parents prior to 1867. Simpson married Mary Elizabeth Smith sometime in early to mid-1867. They probably met and married in Herkimer County, NY. Federal Census records for 1860 show a Mary Smith, 11 years old, living with her 45-year-old mother and sisters in Little Falls, NY. This is the most likely Mary Smith in that area with a birth year of 1848-49. Simpson and Elizabeth's first child, Nathan, was born February 1, 1868. Unfortunately, Elizabeth was to succumb to complications from childbirth as she passed away on February 13, 1868 at the tender age of 20 in Stratford, Fulton County, NY. Simpson was just 22. It is fortuitous that Simpson had his father and mother close by to assist him with his young son.

A year and a day later, on February 14, 1869 Simpson married one of Mary's "most intimate friends", Fanny Case, in Salisbury Center, Herkimer County, NY. This marriage would last for the rest of Simpson's life and yield them three children. Lydia E. McLean was born January 14, 1870 followed shortly by her sister, Alice, born August 4, 1871. Tragedy struck the McLean family on August 20, 1874 when Lydia passed away at the age of 4 years, 7 months, and 6 days. Later, Simpson fathered a son, Russell S., born April 20, 1877.

It is known from the Federal census records and from the testimony of Silas B. Case, the father of Fanny, in her widow's pension application, that the Simpson McLean's resided in and around Stratford and Salisbury, NY, from 1869 to 1895. Federal census records for 1870 carry Simpson as a farmer in Stratford, which is just over the Herkimer County line in Fulton County. The 1870 New York Agricultural Report shows Simpson McLean farming 80 acres with a value of $2,000. That was quite a substantial farm at the time. It is not known if the farm was owned or rented.

In 1880, Simpson is carried on the Federal census records as a farmer residing in Salisbury, Herkimer County. On the census page all three children are noted as is Simpson's father-in-law, Silas B. Case. Case was 53 years old. The New York Agricultural Report for Salisbury, Herkimer County is more specific than the report of ten years earlier. The report shows 38 acres of tilled land, 28 in permanent meadow, and five acres of "other unimproved but not growing wood" for a total of 71 acres. The value of the farm including buildings, machinery, and livestock totaled $1,670. Of this total, the value of the livestock is $385 and the farming implements and machinery as $75. Simpson owned a reasonable amount of livestock; however only $75 of machinery does not seem enough to handle 38 tillable acres. Perhaps Simpson had others working the farm for him while he pursued other endeavors.

Federal Census records for 1890 do not exist as they were destroyed in the previously mentioned fire before being microfilmed. Consequently, little is known about Simpson and his family during this decade. However, New York State conducted a census in 1892. The Salisbury, Herkimer County, portion was recorded on February 16, 1892. Simpson and Fanny are enumerated along with their children Alice and Russell. Silas B. Case is shown on the line above Simpson's name so it can be assumed that the father-in-law of Simpson was still part of the household. Interestingly, Simpson is shown as a merchant while Silas is shown as a laborer same as he was shown in 1880.

By June, 1900, the 73-year-old Silas was living with his daughter, Lydia, and her husband George Hopson. This family also resided in Salisbury. Silas went back to live with Simpson and Fanny at some point as he was living with them in the Ohio Township of Herkimer County at the time of the Federal Census on April 27, 1910. In January, 1920, Silas, now 93, was back living with daughter Lydia Hopson. Silas died in 1921 in Cold Brook, Herkimer County, NY. He lived in Herkimer County his entire life.

For reasons unknown, Simpson McLean is not located on the 1900 Federal Census anywhere within New York State. However, the city directory for Herkimer, NY, in both 1902 and 1904 show Simpson and Russell McLean living at 335 Smith Avenue. Certainly Fanny was at the same address since pension records state that they continually lived as husband and wife. Sometime prior to June 27, 1905, Simpson and Fanny moved 27 miles north to Ohio, NY, on which date Simpson was appointed US Postmaster. He held this position until his death in 1913. The April 27, 1910, Federal census shows Simpson and Fanny residing in the Ohio Township. Also present in the household is Silas Case (83), widowed daughter Alice Morgan (38), 17-year-old grandson Carlton Morgan, and an elderly boarder. Simpson is listed as a merchant and store owner which would be in addition to his being the local postmaster. Simpson was engaged in a variety of endeavors which provided income for the family.

Simpson McLean prospered in the years after the Civil War. The move back to Herkimer County proved to be a good decision. The fact that he could take in his father-in-law and other family members for several years is an indication that he was doing well; certainly better than his relatives. Other internet records mentioning Simpson reveal that he owned the town hall, his store, and meat market in Salisbury Center. In addition, he owned dwellings and lots in Devereaux, NY. Simpson was also a proud member of GAR Post #503 (named after Captain Jonathan Burrell) at Salisbury Center. Unfortunately, most Post records are difficult to come by as there was no national organization for the GAR and thus no central records repository. The post was formed August 4, 1884 and was active until 1912. Simpson's obituary mentions that he was a member of GAR Post #404 named for Sgt. Aaron Helmer, Company G, 34th New York Infantry. Sgt. Helmer was killed at Antietam. This post was chartered September 20, 1883, at Herkimer. Simpson was probably a member of both GAR Posts which was not unusual. It was not possible to determine when Simpson joined either GAR Post nor how long he was active in them. The fact that he was a member of the post indicates that he was proud of his service and wanted to remember it.

Simpson kept track of the benefits the US government offered Civil War veterans. He probably also discussed these benefits with his brother, William. Simpson McLean first applied for an invalid pension on February 13, 1874 at the age of 29. Application records show that he was 5'4-1/2" tall with dark brown hair and gray eyes. A large amount of paperwork substantiated his Gettysburg wound. His initial pension was $3 per month payable beginning January 31, 1874. Additional paperwork submitted in July, 1875, stated that Simpson was 3/8 permanently disabled but this did not result in an increase in his monthly pension. After 12 years, Simpson did apply for an increase in his pension on July 8, 1886. Seven weeks later, the finding by the pension board was that Simpson was now one-half totally disabled. The paperwork also indicates that Simpson was 5'8" tall and weighed 140#. His original enrollment records list his height as 5'4-1/2" tall leading one to believe that his height was incorrectly registered in 1886. The National Archives records are incomplete so it is unknown as to what increase was granted at that time. However, his rate probably increased to $6 per month because that was what he was receiving in March, 1892, when he filed another application for an invalid pension. The extant record states that "He claims a re-rating of his pension on the ground that the rate originally allowed was too low and not commensurate with the extent of his disability, and therefore requests that he be allowed the same rate drawn by others for similar or equivalent disabilities." This demonstrates the extent to which an injured veteran needed to keep track of the records and the payments usually granted for various amounts of disability. The onus was solely on the applicant; nothing was automatic. As a result of this claim, Simpson was granted an increase to $12 per month. Simpson continued to keep up with pension increases as he filed a declaration for an increase on March 7, 1902 and again on May 24, 1912. The National Archives records show he was to receive $19 per month effective May 27, 1912. This was the amount in force at the time of his death in Ohio, NY, on Friday, September 5, 1913, at 7:15 a.m. His death is attributed to heart failure. Simpson was 68 years old. Simpson's severe war wound at Gettysburg surely contributed to his early passing. His older brother, William, outlived him by nine years. Simpson's saga of the Civil War and beyond was now complete.

Two weeks after Simpson's passing, Fanny filed for a widow's pension. Her application is dated September 19, 1913. Her brother-in-law, William J. McLean, himself a civil war veteran and 73 years old at the time, filed a General Affidavit on her behalf dated December 8, 1913. William was living in Utica, NY, at the time. The Affidavit contains some interesting family history which assisted in writing this narrative of Simpson's life. William's affidavit helped Fanny's cause. She was granted a $12 per month pension beginning September 22, 1913. Later, her pension amount was increased to $25 per month retroactive to October 6, 1917. Fanny departed this world on March 26, 1918; only outliving Simpson by four and a half years.

Seated: William J. McLean; Standing: Simpson McLean; taken at Utica, NY, circa 1912. (Source: Ancestry.com).

John C. McLean

Sometime during or after John's service, the family relocated from near Painesville, Ohio, back to the New York state area they once lived. At the time of the June 16, 1870, census recording, John McLean was back living and farming in Stratford, Fulton County, NY. Fulton County is adjacent to Herkimer County on the east and the town of Stratford is just over the Fulton County line. Stratford is also east of Fairfield, where William attended school at the time of his enlistment. John was back in familiar territory and with his family. John and Sarah had two additional children after John returned from his brief military service. The family at home now consisted of John (54), Sarah (43), James (17), Caroline (15), Henry (10), George (8), and one-year-old Lilly Ann (Lillian). By this time, son William had been back in Herkimer County for quite a few years since his discharge from the service in 1863.

The June, 1870, census page reveals that John and his now 30-year-old son, William, lived adjacent to each other as the listing for William follows that of John on the same page. John is listed as a farmer, but his farm was quite small. The value of his real estate is shown as $500 and the value of his personal property is a meager $200. John and Sarah were poor and struggling and probably somewhat supported by his much more prosperous son living next door. William's real estate value was $5,000 and his personal property is listed as $2,000. John and Sarah have the five children listed above living at home with them. On October 22, 1877, John applied for, and received, an invalid pension due to his Civil War service.

The Federal census for June 5, 1880, in Stratford, Fulton County, NY, also carries John and Sarah McLean. John is still farming. Only George (18) and Lillia (10), recorded as Lilly Ann in 1870, remain at home. James, Caroline, and Henry are grown and have left the family home. John and Sarah are no longer living adjacent to William since he is listed on another page. John is shown on page 6 and was the 48th dwelling visited. This indicates he was probably not close to the town area. William and his now larger family is shown on page two and they are the 15th family visited, indicating they are likely in a more developed area. There is no information recorded for this census about the size or value of the farm or property. Again, no Federal census records exist from 1890.

Per the 1900 Federal census, 73-year-old widowed Sarah J. McLean was living on a mortgaged farm with her son George (38), who was employed as a day laborer. The family patriarch, John C. McLean, passed away on January 3, 1894. Just a little over three weeks after the death of John, Sarah applied for a widow's pension on January 27, 1894. She no doubt received this pension. The census records list their farm as being in town of Stratford, Fulton County. It's possible this is the same farm on which they resided in 1880. John and Sarah's son Henry is shown as living in Whitesboro Village, just west of Utica. He is married and has two young daughters. Their son James is not listed in Fulton, Herkimer, or Oneida counties.

A 1913 letter of his son William to the Pension Bureau in regard to his own pension claim, states that his father lived until 1893. However, cemetery records for the Stratford Cemetery, Town of Salisbury, Herkimer County, New York, indicate John C. McLean died in 1894. He is buried with his wife, Sarah J. (Moody) McLean, who died in 1910. Thus, John lived 32 years after his term of service ended and he died at the age of 80.

John McLean was close to his children and knew the circumstances of their lives. This is evidenced by what he wrote in his will dated October 8, 1892. He appointed Simpson, his most successful son, to be his executor along with D. S. Watson (not further identified). John left all of his estate to his wife, Sarah, except for a few items. He previously gave some unnamed possessions to his daughter, Amelia. John left $50 to his daughter, Nancy and his "watch and silver chain" to his grandson, John Woolworth. In an interestingly worded statement in his will, he named his sons William, John, Simpson, James M., Henry W., and George B. and added, "I feel justified in that they are in no need and allow them nothing of my estate." For undetermined reasons, two other children are unnamed, Alexander (born 1847) and Mary (born 1855). They may have been deceased by late 1892.

John C. McLean was a patriot who served his country the best he could. His age and infirmity was against him but nonetheless he wanted to serve his country and did so with dignity and honor.

148   *A Soldier's Life in the Civil War*

Additional Information Regarding Addison Phillips

In Chapter VIII, footnote 125 refers to an African American named Addison Phillips, his wife and child being in the camp of the 34th. How they came to be with the 34th is a story completed by the recently obtained obituary of Addison Phillips. The obituary with photo was provided by Mr. David P. Krutz, the author of *Distant Drums*. Since this information was not available at the writing of *Distant Drums*, it is relevant to be included in this partial history of the 34th New York infantry and thus in the annals of Civil War history for perhaps the first time in 158 years.

It is not remarkable that, when they knew of the Union troops being just across the Potomac River in Maryland, Addison Phillips risked his life and the lives of his family to escape slavery. Many African Americans took the same chance whether singly, in groups, or more rarely as a family unit. However, the Fugitive Slave Act of 1850 was in effect throughout the United States. This controversial law required that fugitive slaves be returned to their masters no matter where in the country they were found. It is a tribute to the officers and men of the 34th New York that this did not happen to the Phillips family. In actuality, other slaves who escaped across the Potomac were either not permitted to land on the Maryland side or were returned to Virginia against their will.

The Saturday Globe was a weekly newspaper in Utica, NY. The newspaper also had a Little Falls edition. Today, Addison Phillips lies forever free in a Little Falls, NY, cemetery.

Obituary in *The Saturday Globe*, Saturday, March 5, 1904

Little Falls, March 4 – With the old soldiers who fought for their liberty are also passing the remnant of former slaves that accompanied our victorious troops north to enter on a new life of freedom and citizenship. Addison Phillips, a familiar figure about Little Falls, dropped dead from heart disease last Tuesday morning while shoveling snow.

ADDISON PHILLIPS.

He was born in Fairfax county, (sic) Virginia, about 1834, and was reared and wedded in slavery, finally making an escape with his family which sounds like romantic fiction. Learning that the northern troops were encamped not far away, he planned with a companion to get away and set about the enterprise in the dead of night. The creaking of the cabin floor was muffled with bed clothing, and the party was to get away part at a time, the men leading. Missing his wife, Addison returned for her and found her paralyzed with terror. He urged her on and with their second child, he having already removed the first, made their way out. It was moonlight, and there in the glow stood a man at a little distance, mutely observant. He did not temp violence from the knife-armed and desperate negro, who never knew whether he was restrained by fear or sympathy, being unable to recognize him farther than to see that he was white. The flight proceeded safely until the Potomac river (sic) was being crossed, when a sleepy northern sentry, suddenly alarmed by the apparition of a white bundle of clothing that occupied the bow of the fugitives' boat, fired into it. No one was hurt and an understanding was soon reached. Phillips fell in with the Thirty-fourth Regiment, composed of Herkimer county men. His courage and willingness attracted the fancy of Col. Esterbrook, to whom he became groom, and at the close of the war he came to Little Falls where he had since resided securing by industry and thrift a little home.

In his prime he was a man of great personal strength. His mother was direct from Africa, and he often told how powerful a woman she was and with what fortitude she could assert her rights on occasion. Deceased is survived by a son and three daughters, all resident elsewhere.

Epilogue

William John McLean, along with his father John and his brother Simpson, answered the call of their President in 1861. Their reasons for entering the service were certainly varied and remain unknown; but yet they did answer the call when many others did not. They served with honor, though not with specific distinction, other than to themselves. Fortunately, though the two brothers were seriously wounded, both the brothers and their father survived the war. It may have been their war experiences which influenced John and Simpson to relocate after the war back to the familiar rural countryside of Herkimer County, New York. Here they were to remain until their deaths.

Over the many ensuing years, they probably shared stories and remembrances with many of their friends who also served. The four Herkimer County regiments ensured that a significant number of soldiers returned and remained in the area. Simpson is the only family member whom we know for sure was active in the Union Veterans organization, the Grand Army of the Republic (GAR). It may be that William and John were as well. It is reasonable to assume that they socialized with their fellow veterans over many years. Although not known for certain, William may have participated in some of the many reunions held by the surviving veterans of the 34th New York Infantry

Reunion Ribbon, September 17, 1918; date is the anniversary of the Battle of Antietam.
(Source: Author's Collection).

such as the 42nd annual reunion held at Herkimer on the 56th anniversary of the Antietam battle.

Their individual stories are not unique in themselves, but taken together they are illustrative of the sacrifices millions of families on both sides made to preserve our American heritage. It can be argued that the country had to go through this terrible conflict among our own people and on our own soil to get to where we are today. Freedom was not free for the McLean family or for those of all other wars. Their contributions were significant and their pain and suffering was continuous. They deserve to be in our memory.

Works Cited And Sources

American Civil War Research Database. Historical Data Systems, Inc. multiple soldier records.

Ancestry.com, multiple individual and family records.

Baltz, John D. *Hon. Edward D. Baker, U.S. Senator from Oregon*. Lancaster, PA: Inquirer Printing Company, 1888.

Catalogue of the Officers and Students of Fairfield Academy at Fairfield, Herkimer Co., N.Y. for the Year Ending July 3, 1861. Albany, New York: S.R. Gray, 1861.

Chapin, L.N. *A Brief History of the Thirty-fourth Regiment N.Y.S.V.* Privately Printed, 1903.

Find-A-Grave.com, multiple individual records.

Google Images.

Harper's Weekly, multiple editions.

Krutz, David P. *Distant Drums, Herkimer County, New York in the War of the Rebellion*. Utica, New York: North Country Books, 1997.

Library of Congress, digital images collection.

Lyon, Henry C. *"Desolating this Fair Country" The Civil War Diary and Letters of Lt. Henry C. Lyon, 34th New York*, ed. Emily N. Radigan. Jefferson, NC: McFarland & Company, Inc., 1999.

McLean, William J. Personal diary, 1861.

McLean, William J., Letters exchanged with the Bureau of Pensions, 1912-1913.

Morgan III, James A. *A Little Short of Boats, The Battles of Ball's Bluff and Edwards Ferry, October 21-22, 1861*. New York, NY: Savas Beatie LLC, 2011.

National Archives and Records Administration, Washington, DC. Military and Pension Records of William J. McLean, Company C, 34th New York Infantry; Simpson McLean, Company F, 29th Ohio Infantry; John C. McLean, Company F, 29th Ohio Infantry.

Urban, Dennis D., personal collection.

Wikipedia, multiple records

About the Author

Dennis D. Urban is a life-long student of the Civil War whose intense interest began in elementary school with a trip to the Gettysburg battlefield with his family and with the reading of a Civil War book about the Andrew's Raiders. He grew up in Takoma Park, MD, a suburb of Washington, DC, and within an hour's drive of many of the significant eastern theater battlefields in Maryland, Virginia, and Pennsylvania. Urban graduated from Archbishop John Carroll High School in Washington, DC, near the site of the Harewood Hospital during the Civil War. He is a 1969 graduate of the University of Maryland, College Park, earning a degree in Secondary Education. Urban is a consummate researcher, collector, and Civil War historian.

Urban is retired from the Oak Ridge Institute of Science and Education, Oak Ridge, TN. He served in the volunteer fire service for 35 years primarily in Montgomery County, MD, where he attained the rank of chief in two departments in the county. He also served as a volunteer and officer in Prince George's County, MD, and Jefferson County, KY.

Mr. Urban is a former president of the Knoxville Civil War Roundtable (2013 – 2016) and he is designated as a Master Local Historian by the East Tennessee Historical Society. He is a speaker to various groups throughout the Knoxville area on the subject of the Civil War history of Knoxville and the divided loyalties of the area residents.

www.ingramcontent.com/pod-product-compliance
Lightning Source LLC
Chambersburg PA
CBHW071431160426
43195CB00013B/1870